Consultations in
Psychoanalytic Psychotherapy

Consultations in Psychoanalytic Psychotherapy

Edited by

R. Peter Hobson

Routledge
Taylor & Francis Group

LONDON AND NEW YORK

First published 2013 by
Karnac Books Ltd.

Published 2019 by Routledge
2 Park Square, Milton Park, Abingdon, Oxon OX14 4RN
52 Vanderbilt Avenue, New York, NY 10017, USA

Routledge is an imprint of the Taylor & Francis Group, an informa business

British Library Cataloguing in Publication Data

A C.I.P. for this book is available from the British Library

ISBN: 9781855757905 (pbk)

Edited, designed, and produced by Communication Crafts

*This book is dedicated to my father, Bob Hobson,
for what we shared and where we diverged, and to
two institutions remarkable for fostering reflective thought:
The Tavistock Clinic, London, and
The Center for Advanced Study in the Behavioral Sciences,
Stanford, California.*

CONTENTS

SERIES EDITOR'S PREFACE

Margot Waddell

Since it was founded in 1920, the Tavistock Clinic has developed a wide range of developmental approaches to mental health which have been strongly influenced by the ideas of psychoanalysis. It has also adopted systemic family therapy as a theoretical model and a clinical approach to family problems. The Clinic is now the largest training institution in Britain for mental health, providing postgraduate and qualifying courses in social work, psychology, psychiatry, and child, adolescent, and adult psychotherapy, as well as in nursing and primary care. It trains about 1,700 students each year in over 60 courses.

The Clinic's philosophy aims at promoting therapeutic methods in mental health. Its work is based on the clinical expertise that is also the basis of its consultancy and research activities. The aim of this Series is to make available to the reading public the clinical, theoretical, and research work that is most influential at the Tavistock Clinic. The Series sets out new approaches in the understanding and treatment of psychological disturbance in children, adolescents, and adults, both as individuals and in families.

Clinical consultation—the capacity to assess what lies behind a referred patient's difficulties and therefore to decide what mode, length, and depth of treatment could be most helpful—constitutes a supremely challenging task. Before now, surprisingly little has been written on the subject.

As Series Editor, I am delighted to be publishing a book that addresses itself to this very challenge. In this sense, *Consultations in Psychoanalytic Psychotherapy* is not only most welcome in the Series itself but is also welcome for its inevitable appeal to other professionals in different settings. For it articulates, in a variety of voices, a distillation of the experience of the Adult Department at the Tavistock Clinic—its wisdom and its expertise in the particular area of the consultation process. What is happening psychodynamically? Where is this clinical encounter going? What might be its outcome, and how might that be determined? The editor and contributors, among the most eminent in the field, address such questions and many more. All seem to have a gift for writing vividly and accessibly. Overall these pages are refreshingly free of jargon, but where it is needed—as in the concepts, for example, of transference and countertransference, or of projective identification—the terms are described with unusual clarity.

The cohering thread, which is approached from different angles and points of view, is that of how to enable patients, during these brief encounters, to make sense of what is happening to them and how better they may integrate different parts of themselves. At the core of this is, as Peter Hobson says, "the pursuit of truth". What evidence, he asks, is relevant for arriving at a potentially correct or incorrect view of a person's psychological functioning? With authority and with scholarly accuracy, the contributors examine the inter-personal and intra-personal dynamics that could be described as epitomizing this kind of work. But they also draw on the research perspective and on the developmental, the institutional, and the broader cultural and political contexts, each of which has a significant bearing on the work.

This is a very special kind of encounter, and Hobson is unstintingly honest about the complexities of such a clinical endeavour, springing alive—as it does—usually from a bare referral letter. In a sense, the pages interrogate what can possibly rise to the surface in so short a time, in the course of what might seem so limited an engagement. But rise to the surface things do—a mysterious process to which these pages so richly attest. *Consultations in Psychoanalytic Psychotherapy* is a model of insight and exposition.

ABOUT THE EDITOR AND CONTRIBUTORS

David Bell is a Consultant Psychiatrist in Psychotherapy and Director of the Fitzjohn's Unit, a service for patients with complex needs including personality disorder, based in the Tavistock Clinic. He is a training and supervising psychoanalyst of the British Psychoanalytical Society and has just stood down from being its President. He is Professorial Fellow at Birkbeck College, University of London.

Ruth Berkowitz is a psychoanalyst (British Psychoanalytical Association) and a psychoanalytic psychotherapist (British Association of Psychotherapists). She has written papers on assessment in both primary care and forensic settings. She worked as a Consultant Adult Psychotherapist at the Portman Clinic from 2002 to 2011 and is now in full-time private practice.

Antony Garelick is a Consultant Psychiatrist in Psychotherapy at the Tavistock & Portman NHS Trust and North East London Mental Health Trust, and Associate Dean, London Deanery. He is Head of the Tavistock Clinic MedNet Service, which is a confidential service for doctors in difficulty.

R. Peter Hobson is Tavistock Professor of Developmental Psycho-pathology in the University of London. He is a psychoanalyst in the British Psychoanalytical Society, Honorary Consultant Psychiatrist in Psychotherapy at the Tavistock Clinic, and a research professor at the Institute of Child Health, University College London. His previous books include *The Cradle of Thought* (2002), in which he combines psychoanalytic thinking with developmental research.

Raman Kapur, MBE, is Chief Executive, Consultant Clinical Psychologist & Psychoanalytic Psychotherapist with the mental health charity THRESHOLD in Northern Ireland. He was formerly Course Director of the MSc in Psychoanalytic Psychotherapy at Queen's University Belfast. In addition to papers on psychotherapy, he has published a book on the emotional effects of the troubles in Northern Ireland.

Birgit Kleeberg is a Consultant Adult Psychotherapist. Her experience with more troubled patients comes from having worked at the Cassel Hospital and from managing the Fitzjohn's Unit, a service for patients with complex needs, based in the Tavistock Clinic.

Karlen Lyons-Ruth is a Professor of Psychology in the Department of Psychiatry at Harvard Medical School and a supervising psychologist at the Cambridge Hospital. Her research has focused on the assessment of attachment relationships in high-risk environments, and she is currently examining interaction patterns that distinguish young borderline patients and their parents from other diagnostic groups.

Jane Milton is a psychiatrist and a training analyst of the British Psychoanalytical Society. Much of her experience in NHS assessments was gained at the Maudsley Hospital Psychotherapy Department and in the Adult Department of the Tavistock Clinic. Currently she has a special interest in the development of psychoanalysis in Ukraine.

Matthew Patrick is Chief Executive of the Tavistock and Portman NHS Foundation Trust. Originally trained as an adult psychiatrist, for many years he combined clinical work and developmental research. He is also a training and supervising analyst for the British Psychoanalytical Society.

Joanne Stubley is a Consultant Psychiatrist in Psychotherapy at the Tavistock Clinic. She leads the Adult Section of the Tavistock Trauma Service, which offers a variety of therapeutic packages to treat single-episode as well as complex and developmental trauma. She is a member of the British Psychoanalytical Society.

PART I

INTRODUCTION

I begin by offering an overview of the book and then discuss the aims and rationale of consultations in psychoanalytic psychotherapy. For those unfamiliar with psychoanalytic concepts, I conclude with a brief explanation of terms that will crop up in the ensuing chapters.

CHAPTER 1

Overview

R. Peter Hobson

Psychotherapy practice within the National Health Service presents few more exacting clinical tasks than to conduct a psychoanalytic consultation interview. In the case of consulting with an adult individual—and it is with this kind of interview, rather than meetings with children, couples, or families, that the present book is concerned—a principal aim is to discern the nature of and basis for someone's emotional difficulties and assess the person's potential to benefit from one or another kind of psychotherapy. Yet beneath this seemingly simple description there lie formidable complexities.

Consider how the meeting between two people, initially strangers to one another, is convened. Sometimes the therapist who encounters a person for the first time is forewarned and forearmed by a referral letter penned by a time-starved family doctor. Sometimes the therapist also has the benefit of the patient's own best efforts to respond (or not) to a personal if straight-laced questionnaire. On other occasions, the therapist has almost nothing to which he or she can cling as the moment of interview approaches. In any case, whether clear-etched or shadowy, fulsome or sparse, background information affords little to the therapist by way of protection or foresight. The only real preparation is to anticipate being unprepared. The consultation will yield what it will. Anything could happen.

What is so alarming and remarkable about all this is that in the space of 90 minutes, deep and serious intimacies may be achieved or steadfastly avoided, profound griefs or resentments articulated or denied, sorrows and losses pinpointed or evaded, lifelong traumata revived or reviewed, and the most personal of relationships recounted or relived. Whatever does happen is hugely significant for the two people involved. This book illustrates as much.

If all this is so, then wherein lies the challenge of conducting assessment consultations? It sounds like falling off a log—into a turbulent river, perhaps, but falling nevertheless. Yet beyond the need to keep one's head above water, one has the job of charting often unstable currents of emotion in the patient's relationships, including emotions towards the patient's own self, in order to achieve an adequate grasp of the problems and envisage the prospects for psychotherapy. And as we shall see, appraising what is important for a person's difficulties and distress is just one dimension of a multifaceted therapeutic endeavour that has the aims not only of understanding the patient, but also (and partly through this) of embarking on the task of promoting the patient's *development* through disorder and distress to more fruitful functioning.

This book emerged from discussions that took place in 2008–9 within a clinical unit (chaired by Cyril Couve and subsequently Julian Lousada) in the Adult Department of the Tavistock Clinic. We found that when different clinicians presented distilled accounts of assessment consultations, we learnt a great deal not only about therapists' professional endeavours and patients' emotional and relationship difficulties, but also about the *various* processes through which "assessment" may be accomplished. The clinicians involved were psychodynamic psychotherapists, all of whom believed in the value of tracing how a patient's conflicts become manifest in the relationship with the therapist in the transference. Again and again this proved to be an important avenue to achieving depth in understanding. Yet each clinician was distinctive in how he or she began the interview, steadied proceedings or prompted the patient–therapist exchanges to move forward, and conceptualized the prime focus and goal of the meeting.

At the outset, I had hoped to chart some of these differences in therapeutic orientation and practice through diverse chapters written by an assortment of therapists who would then compare and contrast their respective approaches. For a variety of reasons, this hope was not fulfilled. I mention this because it is important to appreciate that there is no single correct way to conduct psychodynamic consultations. It is neither helpful nor justified to prescribe in detail how a therapist should behave. Provided that care is taken to respect a patient's needs for confidentiality and interpersonal boundaries are maintained, there may be many ways to proceed. What is most appropriate and helpful for one therapist in relation to one patient may be inappropriate and unhelpful for another therapist with another patient. We do not have agreed criteria for what is to count as effective when it comes to psychoanalytic consultations. Even if we did, still we lack adequate research to justify claims that such criteria are met by one approach and not another.

In the event, then, this book represents not so much diversity in therapeutic attitude and technique as, rather, the working-over of ideas pertaining to a more restricted, and perhaps distinctive, style of assessment consultation. However, what the book lacks in variety, it may compensate for through relative consistency. Yet this is only one take on its contents, because contrasts in approach are also in evidence. Even to the degree that there is consensus on the purpose and some of the techniques of consultation, both the aims and the application of techniques need to be modified in keeping with the different settings in which consultations take place.

Another feature of the book is that it comprises chapters that differ in style as well as content. Readers should be prepared for some choppy transitions from one chapter to the next. Consultations are being considered from distinct vantage-points, and each contributor has written in a style that suits his or her communicative purpose. This chapter provides a point of orientation. At the beginning of Part II, Ruth Berkowitz gives an academically rich account of the historical background to our theme, and readers wishing to consult the literature will find in her chapter prominent works summarized and signposted (for which one might also consult books edited by Cooper & Alfillé, 1998, and by Mace, 1995). Jane Milton follows in chapter 3 with a deeply thoughtful discussion on the conduct and rationale of psychoanalytic consultations. The authors of Parts III and IV—respectively, myself and then Joanne Stubley, Dave Bell, and Birgit Kleeberg—mostly draw on first-hand clinical experience, albeit with respectful reference to inspirational thinkers, rather than discuss and critique the ideas of others. We trust readers will appreciate that although there are many other works that are not mentioned, this in no way signifies that the contributions of others are undervalued, nor that we are seeking to appropriate the original ideas and clinical accounts on which much of our thinking has been founded. Finally, Part V starts with a chapter by colleagues and myself, on research reflections. Here we do not attempt to review such scant evidence as exists on the predictive validity of assessment interviews. Instead, and in keeping with what has gone before, we describe illustrative research studies to complement the clinical experience of psychotherapists and to inform interested parties within and beyond psychiatry and clinical psychology. Antony Garelick rounds things off in his chapter by considering the changing times in which psychoanalytic psychotherapists carry on consulting.

We have taken pains to secure patients' permission to present disguised clinical material. In rare instances, identities have been reconfigured by mixing together clinical material from two or more individuals. In every case, we have tried to capture what happened in the process of consultation.

The book's primary aim, then, is to illustrate clinical, psychoanalytic approaches to understanding people in depth, even when breadth of understanding is severely constricted by the brevity of a consultation. If the book is successful in this aim, then it will also reveal the limitations of much that passes under the rubric of "psychological therapies" in contemporary NHS practice—which is not at all to diminish the potential value of such treatments. In-depth understanding is neither necessary nor sufficient to promote a person's mental health, and here there is no claim (nor even discussion of the claim) that the psychodynamic approach is superior to non-psychodynamic assessments or interventions in diagnosing or resolving emotional distress. It is not superior—but it does have the power to reach parts of a person's mind that other approaches only sense.

The what and why of assessment consultations

There is a fuzzy boundary between assessment consultations and the kinds of session that take place in brief or even longer term psychoanalytic psychotherapy. To be sure, there are a number of contrasts that could be highlighted, not least because the therapeutic engagement between an assessing psychotherapist and a patient is brief in nature. For example, my standard practice for such consultations is to have a preliminary meeting that lasts 90 minutes and one or two follow-up meetings, each lasting about 40 minutes. Of course, the assessment will need to accomplish things—from introducing a person to the experience of psychotherapy to excluding biological forms of psychiatric disorder—that do not feature in routine psychotherapy. Having said this, I want to bring out potential similarities between brief and lengthier psychotherapeutic encounters.

I take the view that even one-off assessment consultations are comparable to longer periods of psychotherapy in having a beginning, a middle, and an end; they can draw upon techniques that are much the same as those involved in a more extended psychotherapeutic relationship; and they serve therapeutic aims. If the term "assessment" implies that the therapist is the one assessing, then it captures only part of the truth. Consultations are also for the patient to assess the therapist's qualities, the nature and potential relevance of psychoanalytic therapy, and what the demands and implications of psychotherapy might be. Last but not least, they allow the patient to discover whether or not he or she wishes to engage in this form of treatment.

Some patients seek the kinds of self-exploration and discovery that psychotherapy makes possible, others do not. It is a central task of assessment consultations to confront this issue. It is also important that potential benefits and risks of entering or not entering treatment are addressed in an explicit manner. At the end of the day, patients need to be in a position to decide whether, if treatment is offered, they accept or decline the offer.

Not infrequently at the beginning of a consultation, a patient will ask what psychotherapy is. I tend to reply that this is an important question that, of course, the patient has a right to ask, and perhaps we can return to it later. In such cases, I make a point of coming back to the question near the conclusion of the interview. When I do so, I express doubt whether it would be helpful for me to give a worked-out description of what psychotherapy is. I say I believe that in the course of our meeting, the patient has had first-hand experience of what it involves. I also say that this kind of experience is what should enable the patient to tell how dynamic psychotherapy may or may not be relevant for his or her difficulties.

It remains the responsibility of the therapist to make a judgement whether, in the balance of probabilities, psychotherapeutic treatment of a particular kind—whether individual or group or family therapy, whether conducted by a novice or an experienced therapist, whether brief or lengthy, whether NHS or private, whether psychodynamic or non-dynamic, whether set up as a stand-alone venture or coordinated with other (e.g., psychiatric) services—will serve the patient's best interests. Will such treatment be acceptable to the patient, is it likely that the patient will work through difficult times and stay the course, and will the therapy promote development and thereby change the person's emotional life? On the other side of the equation, is there a significant danger that treatment will make things worse? These questions will resurface in ensuing parts of the book.

Very often, it is helpful to arrange one or more follow-up interviews, to see how the initial consultation has taken. What emerges then will inform a therapist's conclusions over the critical question: does this person have the wish and ability to partake in, and benefit from, treatment of the kind offered, and does he or she know what this may entail? It also gives the patient an opportunity to review what has happened, and to communicate his or her feelings, negative as well as positive, to the person of the therapist. Sometimes I have said to patients that I am sorry that they found parts of the first consultation stressful or distressing, and I have meant this. By now, this communication is in the context of mutual understanding that patient and therapist needed to get hold of elusive but vitally important aspects of the person's emotional life.

And finally, of course, the therapist has the job of accommodating his or her view of what the patient needs to the realities of what might be available. It is shorthand to think in terms of generic treatment, for the reason that much depends on the experience and skill of the therapist who is to conduct the treatment. Once patient and therapist have come to a shared view on what might be optimal, taking such realities into consideration, then the therapist does his or her best to move towards this goal, either through arranging something with the patient or giving the patient advice.

The patient–therapist relation

It is easy enough to catalogue some of the principal aims of conducting a psychodynamic assessment interview. It is less easy to accomplish them. How is one to achieve what one needs to achieve for the patient, and indeed for the system (often including the NHS) within which the patient is embedded?

Among the most important qualities a therapist brings to a consultation, two stand out. First, the therapist has a serious commitment to trying to understand the patient in a personal way. Second, the therapist has the aim of communicating this understanding as and when it is appropriate for promoting the patient's development.

To some, this statement will seem anodyne. Yet such a therapeutic orientation and attitude may be contrasted with other approaches that stress the importance of putting a patient at ease, offering supportive comments, providing information and reassurance, taking a detailed developmental and psychiatric history, evolving a life narrative, or even achieving empathy. It is not that these modes of therapeutic contact are unimportant, and each may well have a place in any given encounter. For instance, there are times when what emerges during a consultation requires that time is set aside at the end, or in an alternative interview, for a thorough psychiatric appraisal. Yet despite this, I would put at the very top of the list what I have just described as a therapist's commitment to understanding the patient in a personal way, aligned with the aim of fostering the patient's development.

What, then, do such things mean? In trying to understand a patient, a therapist is after the *truth*. In my view, this means much more (though also, at times, much less) than creating a coherent narrative, or seeing things from a patient's point of view. It means striving to characterize what is the case, or what is objectively true, of this person. What is true in this sense includes what is true of the patient's emotional (psychic) reality, of course. As a therapist, one may not have the means to prove that what one concludes *is* true in this way—that is, to establish that anyone in a position to make an accurate judgement would agree with oneself over a particular formulation of a particular patient's emotional difficulties. But this does not gainsay the importance of striving for an account that has truth as its *raison d'être*.

This orientation is one that pervades the therapeutic work. It is not just that the therapist is trying to find out what is true of the patient. It is also that much of the communication between therapist and patient is addressed to *determining* the truth, either directly or indirectly. So, too, much communication is addressed to analysing the facts of how the patient (and sometimes the therapist) are drawn to deflect from the truth or from truth-revealing inter-personal engagement, or imposing non-truths, in order to manage distress, conflict, and pain.

In case all this is too abstract, let me give a brief illustration. It has been said that when a therapist finds that he or she is avoiding or failing to address something that is happening in relation to a patient, then that is precisely the matter that the therapist needs to find a way of making explicit. If the therapist cannot manage to address things squarely (in an appropriate way, of course—blurt-ing things out is not "managing"), then it is likely that neither will the patient be enabled to do so. Or, to take a less weighty example, consider the therapist who steals surreptitious glances at his or her watch to see how long before the session ends, or who finds he or she cannot raise the issue of the next break. It is not just that such attempts to conceal or evade uncomfortable or conflict-ridden ele-ments of truth are ultimately fruitless. Far more important, they undermine the very foundations of psychodynamic psychotherapy. Psychotherapy is not only about the pursuit of truth. It is constantly and unremittingly orientated towards the truth. This is so, even when therapist and patient explore how facing the truth and reality is too difficult to bear.

Certain implications flow from this way of looking at the psychoanalytic encounter. Here I shall focus on the implications for a therapist's attitude and technique, rather than those that pertain to the patient's mental health.

First, a hallmark of the pursuit of truth is respect for evidence. What evidence is relevant for arriving at a potentially correct or incorrect view of a person's psychological functioning? Second, what *kinds* of account of the patient might be justified by the evidence that is available to a therapist?

My answers to these rhetorical questions are framed by a view of the method or procedure of psychoanalytic psychotherapy. This view is not shared by all psychotherapists. It combines a relatively restricted focus on that concerning which a therapist *has* strong evidence—namely, what is happening here and now between patient and therapist—and severe requirements for evidence of what the therapist takes to be happening in the to-and-fro engagement. To be sure, a therapist's acts of judgement will be influenced and informed by ideas derived from theory or drawn from prior experience. But at the end of the day, any formulation of a patient's difficulties that arises out of a therapeutic consultation needs to be justified by evidence derived from current patient–therapist transactions.

What, then, is the nature of this evidence—and how does all this tie up with the need for a therapist to understand a patient in a "personal" way?

Classes of evidence

Many kinds of fact are relevant for understanding a person's life situation. There are facts about the person's current, past, and potential future relationships, perhaps especially about intimate and supportive and/or conflictual relationships; facts about the person's circumstances, including the kinds of fact (age, gender, race, religion) of interest to sociologists; facts about the person's living conditions, including housing and financial situation; facts about the person's current and past medical and psychiatric history, and perhaps that of his or her relatives; and, of course, the relations among each of these and other groupings of fact, and the person's aspirations, disappointments, frustrations, and so on in the context of his or her phase of life.

Even these kinds of fact may not be easy to establish. However, no one would dispute their status as "facts", nor their potential relevance for understanding a person. A therapeutic consultation may well require that one evaluates any number of these characteristics, often through specific enquiry in the final phase of a consultation.

Then there is a second class of fact, one that sometimes blurs into the first. These are the facts concerning what a patient writes (perhaps in a questionnaire), says, or otherwise indicates to be the case. Sometimes one can feel confident in the veracity of such "patient reports", and in any case it is important to accord these accounts respect as communicating *something* relevant about the patient. Although the content may provide valuable information, this information is always selected and shaped by what is or has been meaningful for the patient. It is suffused with the patient's experience of whatever is reported, sometimes explicitly ("I felt my mother didn't really love me, but I don't know if that was true", or "I feel I cannot be trusted in matters of the heart"), and often implicitly. One might surmise that this class of fact—perhaps it is a stretch to call it a class—ranges from accounts of objective reality to more or less direct verbal expressions of psychic reality, sometimes unconscious reality. What status should one give to the content of a dream that a patient reports, for example?

A third class of fact is especially important in psychodynamic consultations. These are facts of how the patient engages with the therapist, as well as with the patient him/herself. Of course, one might say that such relations, too, express unconscious phantasy (where "phantasy" refers to a largely unconscious inner world of personal relations, to be illustrated at various points in the book). And indeed they do. But there is something special about the nature of the evidence on which one draws to arrive at judgements about interpersonal engagement that is special, whether or not one is focusing on the "unconscious phantasy" part of what is happening.

The evidence is special by virtue of its source in the unique qualities of *intersubjective engagement*. At the most basic level, we apprehend and come to understand the nature of persons and people's mental states through our emotional engagements *with* persons and the attitudes they express. This is something that I have explored from an epistemological viewpoint, in part through the study of autism (e.g., R. P. Hobson, 1993), and a matter that my father Bob Hobson has discussed in his book *Forms of Feeling* (R. F. Hobson, 1985). The fact that we experience people differently from things is one with far-reaching consequences for our knowledge of the nature of people-with-minds. We know that people have minds, and it is a fact that we know this fact. We do not have a "theory" of minds, as current fashion in psychological theorizing would have us believe. What is important for psychotherapy is that from this starting-point, one can elaborate in much more detail how it is that at any given moment, one person's subjective experience is so intimately and complexly linked with that of a communicative partner.

The psychotherapeutic encounter is framed in order to give the psychotherapist the best chance to register and understand his or her subjective experience in relation to a patient. The setting (including the therapist's technique) does more than this—for instance, in providing boundaries that help protect both patient and therapist from acting out—but the framework is essential if the therapist is going to be able to *relate to his or her own relation with the patient*. In subsequent chapters, I shall illustrate what this means. The nub is that the psychotherapist needs *both* to become implicated in how a particular patient shapes the patient–therapist engagement, *and* to be semi-detached from, and yet in touch with, the therapist's own emotional stance. Only in this way can the therapist analyse the countertransference—that is, the therapist's emotional response to what the patient is feeling and doing in the present moment of the relationship—in order better to understand the patient.

Therefore, the third class of fact encompasses the intersubjective goings-on between patient and therapist. It may be a matter of fact that a therapist comes to *feel* inadequate with one patient, amazingly insightful with another, and just about good enough with a third. It may be a matter of fact that a therapist becomes passionately concerned for one patient, bored with another, and fearful in relation to a third. These are facts about the patient–therapist relationship—or, I would prefer to say, about patient–therapist relatedness as this evolves—and they are hugely relevant for understanding the patient.

In passing, I would like to point out that this has implications for training psychotherapists. There is much to gain from seeing at least two patients, even at the beginning of one's life as a psychotherapist. Soon one learns that different patients press different emotional buttons. Yes, one's experience is one's own experience, but what one thinks and feels as a therapist can be intimately connected with what a patient is experiencing, as well as needing the therapist to experience, at any given moment in a session.

The nature of interpersonal understanding has implications that extend beyond the domain of "diagnosis". The reason is that the therapist's intent to strive for and sometimes achieve an appropriate *form* of understanding may be vitally important for meeting a patient's immediate as well as developmental needs.

The following is perhaps to state the obvious, but it is worth stating anyway. There is a fact of human psychology that is so commonplace as to be taken for granted: we need to be listened to and understood. A vivid example of what this means is a toddler's response to parental care. A 1-year-old boy falls and hurts his knee. He turns to an emotionally unreceptive parent, and the hurt and distress continue unabated. Another 1-year-old falls and hurts his knee. He turns to an emotionally receptive parent, one who registers his distress and potential humiliation, and shows age-appropriate sympathy laced with encouragement to battle on. Lo!, the boy's hurt and distress resolve. With the application of a band-aid to assist a working-through process, the boy returns to play. This boy's *development* has been fostered, and not merely his development over the 5 minutes of this episode.

Communication and thinking

There are less obvious dimensions to the processes of understanding and being understood. After all, there are different kinds of communication. This means that the very nature of understanding and being understood may alter not only from one patient to another, but also from one moment to another within a given session. Sometimes, a patient needs to be heard and can register when a therapist is really listening in a personal way; sometimes a patient needs to be rid of certain difficult states of mind and can register when a therapist is able or not able to tolerate what the patient is engendering in the therapist, emotionally speaking; sometimes a patient is communicating his or her own wish that the therapist confront issues (such as the patient's evasiveness) that the patient cannot tackle alone; and so on.

From a complementary perspective, there are a range of difficulties that patients may have in recognizing a therapist's understanding *as* understanding. It can be a frustrating and at times poignant impasse when a therapist's efforts to convey understanding are met with incomprehension or a kind of blank "so what?" There are patients who either cannot feel understood, however sensitive the therapist, or whose feelings of connectedness are so transient that they make little difference to the patients' state and provide an inadequate basis for development. This may occur because a person does not have the wherewithal to register understanding. Alternatively, if being understood is too threatening to the person's identity, or if it stirs too much envy towards the therapist as the source of understanding, then a patient may attack and dissipate potential feelings of being understood. One task of a therapeutic consultation is to address the nature and the sources of such difficulties and assess the prospects for change.

The developmental side of the picture is that interpersonal understanding has remarkable transformational power. It is a principle of development that from early infancy, human beings develop *through* others. Indeed, it is only from one point of view that we exist as individuals. As Winnicott (1964) wrote, there is no such thing as a baby. As individuals, we exist as elements within social *systems*, whether the system of self in relation to another person, or the system of self within a family and more extensive social networks.

If we focus on the system of self in relation to other, there are many properties of the system that depend on the participation of both parties. Moreover, the *development* of each person involved in the relation is dependent on the other. There are a variety of ways in which this is the case. Most important for the present purposes is the principle of what psychoanalysts and the developmental psychologist Vygotsky (1978) called internalization. In elaborating his notion of identifying-with, Freud (1921c, pp. 105–110) stressed how one person *assimilates* the psychological attitudes and characteristics of other people towards the world, including attitudes towards the person's own self. In so doing, the individual's personality is progressively enriched and/or impoverished, depending on what is internalized. Therefore what are first experienced as interpersonal transactions become patterns of relatedness within the individual's own mind—so-called internal object relations. These are then re-lived interpersonally, most notably in the context of a person's intimate relationships. In psychoanalytic psychotherapy, they become accessible as these same patterns are "transferred" on to the person of the psychotherapist (see chapter 7 for a detailed clinical example).

Just now I made passing mention of the Russian developmentalist Lev Vygotsky. In an essay entitled: "Internalization of Higher Psychological Functions", Vygotsky wrote as follows:

> Every function in the child's cultural development appears twice: first, on the social level, and later, on the individual level; first, *between* people (*interpsychological*), and then *inside* the child (*intrapsychological*). This applies equally to voluntary attention, to logical memory, and to the formation of concepts. All the higher functions originate as actual relations between human individuals. [Vygotsky, 1978, pp. 56–57; italics in original]

Therefore, in relation to cognitive as well as emotional development, there is constant interplay between what is individual and what is interpersonal. At any given time, an individual shapes what happens in the interpersonal arena—in a psychotherapy setting, this constitutes the transference—and at the same time, what happens interpersonally can have a profound effect on a person's intrapsychic development.

Thinking in clinical context

Not surprisingly, there has been extensive clinical and theoretical work on the therapeutic action of psychoanalysis. For the present purposes, I highlight three major themes.

First, there is a long tradition of psychoanalytic and psychotherapeutic writing on the significance of symbolic functioning for an individual's emotional and psychological integrity. The most moving and eloquent expression of the idea comes not from Freud but from Shakespeare's *Macbeth*, where Malcolm enjoins the distraught Macduff:

> Give sorrow words. The grief that does not speak
> Whispers the o'er-fraught heart, and bids it break.

Freud considered that finding words for what is unverbalized—and by implication, achieving the insight that may come with the act of giving verbal expression to experience—is critically important if "remembering" is to offer patients release from the compulsion to repeat maladaptive patterns of relatedness.

However, there is a complication here. There are times when what *seem* like instances of symbolic functioning have neither the qualities nor the psychological benefits of mature symbolizing. A well-known instance of this is in the concrete thinking of some people, when symbols have neither the flexibility nor linkages with other symbols that are the hallmark of mature thought. Instead, these individuals may work with what Segal (1957) called symbolic equations. In chapter 8, Joanne Stubley discusses this in relation to patients who have suffered trauma. Perhaps more generally, it is worth appreciating that there is a range of mental operations, from concrete thinking to flexible creative forms of symbolic imagination and thought, which vary in the degree to which they carry emotional meaning and connectedness with other thoughts. They may also differ in how effectively they link the different parts of someone's personality. The aims of therapy are not merely to give words to unmanageable feelings, but also to promote development in how those words become meaningful and afford thinking.

Second, there is the central significance of interpersonal communication. Symbols, including words, are more than vehicles of thought. They develop through interpersonal communication, and of course they mediate much communication. This is the case for intrapsychic as well as interpersonal communication. Segal (1957) linked impairments in symbolizing with dysfunction in interpersonal relations and, more specifically, with a person's mode of locating parts of him/herself and his or her own capacities of mind in another person. The flipside of this is that changes in interpersonal relations fostered by psychotherapy may lead to new ways of thinking, or even the emergence of a new apparatus *for* thinking.

These are matters over which Bion (1962) has made influential contributions. In particular, Bion has explored how the development of the capacity to think (alpha function), rather than to expel elements of experience that are not amenable to thinking (beta elements), depends upon an infant having certain kinds of interpersonal experience. The infant needs to experience his or her caregiver as receptive to what the infant finds unmanageable (including "nameless dread"), in order that the infant can receive back such feelings, now digested by the caregiver, in a manageable, contained form. What is true for infants is also true for many adult psychotherapy patients. In order for a patient to assimilate and come to manage the unmanageable, he or she has to experience *the therapist* as able to deal with the mental contents in question—that is, experiences such as those of not-knowing, dread, or aggression. More than this, the patient needs to find that a therapist can reflect on such contents, sometimes in the face of the patient's own intrusive and emotionally provocative behaviour.

Of course, not all patients are provocative or controlling. Britton (1998) makes the intriguing suggestion that "the need for agreement is inversely proportional to the expectation of understanding" (p, 57). What he means by this is that an individual who expects to be misunderstood, or, in the most troubled cases, to have one's existence threatened, is someone who desperately needs others to agree with his or her view of himself or herself and the world. No doubt, no differences in view are tolerated. The person must impose his or her view or submit to that of the other. When someone like this comes to a consultation, the therapist needs to have a sense of what underlies the urgency and insistence of the patient's communication. Other patients are more receptive, of course, and the therapist has more room to think and explore. The therapist may even find that his or her efforts to understand the patient are received with gratitude and relief.

To complement the above account, Britton (1998) conceives of the acquisition and maintenance of mental space as dependent upon a child's willingness to accept his or her parents' relations with one another, where at times those relations exclude the child him/herself. A person needs to bear the conflicts engendered by

being and moving within triangular sets of relations. This perspective enriches a psychotherapist's view of what patients may need
help in tolerating, not least the psychotherapist's own right to
engage freely in dialogue within his or her own mind.

The overarching principle is that what is unbearable for one
person may become bearable if another person pitches in. True,
humankind cannot bear very much reality, but two humans can
bear a whole lot more than one alone. More than this, there are
circumstances when, once the two together have borne and made
sense of a piece of emotional reality, this becomes manageable for
each within the orbits of their separable minds.

To recap: the first developmental principle I outlined had to do
with constructing and deploying symbolic vehicles of thought. The
second principle had to do with the interpersonal bases for such
construction and deployment. These bases exist on several levels,
from the most fundamental containing function emphasized by
Bion (1962), to the more familiar expressive ("give sorrow words")
level of articulating experience.

A third principle is connected with the second. This concerns a
species of change best promoted from *within* a person's repeating
patterns of relatedness. In the transference, a therapist becomes
implicated in a patient's occurrent phantasies and thereby assumes
a privileged position from which to intervene.

Freud (1912b) described how analysts need to tackle obstacles to
change as these appear in the here-and-now of the psychoanalytic
session. Strachey (1934) took up this theme in his reflections on
the ingredients of a "mutative interpretation". One might imagine
that the lesson has been learnt. Why labour the importance of the
transference and of working with what a patient lives out in relation to the therapist in the present moment?

As we illustrate in chapter 10, there is no consensus on what
it means to work in the transference. This is an understatement.
For instance, there are *very* different ways to construe the nature
of transference-based interpretations. One person's psychoanalytic
psychotherapist is another person's supportive counsellor.

At least let us see what is at stake. Imagine a male patient who is
experiencing the therapist as untrustworthy and insensitive to the
patient's state of mind. The patient is doing his best to disguise that
this is how he feels, perhaps from himself as well as the therapist.

The therapist says: "You are speaking to me as if you trust me to listen to you. In fact, I think you doubt very much whether I am interested in how you feel." The important thing here is that at the very moment that the patient is mistrustful of the therapist's understanding, the patient experiences the therapist as understanding and, moreover, as understanding the patient's mistrust.

This is very different from when patient and therapist talk about the patient's mistrust of, say, colleagues at work, and then the therapist suggests that perhaps the patient has the same kinds of feeling towards the therapist. Here we do not know how the patient is currently experiencing the therapist, and the therapist is inviting a kind of intellectual examination of two situations, one in which the patient relates to colleagues and the other in which the patient relates to the therapist. At times, this may be of value. However, it is not the same as when, at one and the same time, the therapist is being experienced in incompatible ways—for instance, as unreceptive and receptive. In this latter case, there is immediacy to a therapeutic communication that encompasses the emotional facts of the current exchange. Such containment can be important in fostering the capacity to think.

Final thoughts

I have emphasized that both patient and therapist need to be in a position to "assess" in the course of a consultation (see also chapter 3). This does not mean they have the same or equal roles in assessing the patient's suitability for treatment. The patient needs to assess whether he or she wants what psychoanalytic psychotherapy has to offer. But it is the therapist's responsibility to decide whether or not the offer is made.

I shall, in due course, come to consider how to manage the ending of a consultation, whatever its outcome. For the moment, I would like to say that, where possible, a therapist might hope to end the assessment with a kind of rapprochement. If this includes mutual acknowledgement of what has happened in the session for good or ill, then so much the better. Yet this should not be achieved by the therapist forsaking what he or she believes to be the case about the patient and his or her difficulties. The therapist will respect the patient's views and decisions, but does not need to agree with them. This, too, is a mark of respect, not only for the patient but for the status and significance of psychic reality.

Finally for now, I want to note some ethical issues that have emerged. Is it ethical to involve patients in a painful and potentially disturbing process such as a psychoanalytic assessment interview? Clearly, some form of patient consent is vital. One does not do psychotherapy unless there is a contract to do so, any more than one performs surgery unless a patient has given agreement to the procedure. Yet how can someone consent to an assessment prior to knowing what the process will entail? On the other hand, how can a person gain information that is really informative without experiencing something of what happens in an assessment? It is also of great value when unexpected elements in the assessment give spontaneity and depth to the relational processes that unfold.

There is no choice but to strive for a balance among competing demands. Yes, the patient should be provided with information, and questionnaires are a potent way of communicating what the therapist will consider important. Yes, consent must be sought. At the same time, if a patient is going to need a deep and weighty consultation—and a therapist should aim at nothing less—then this will mean that *direct* evidence should emerge over the patient's strengths and vulnerabilities, and positive and negative attitudes, in relation to future psychotherapy. Assessment consultations can be stormy as well as searching. In one sense, they may need to be. They are not to be taken lightly, by either party.

Postscript: some notes on terminology

We are hoping that this book will be accessible to people outside the psychotherapy profession as well as to psychotherapists. Therefore, we have tried to keep technical jargon to a minimum. Having said this, certain ideas are so important in psychoanalytic theory that it would be unhelpful to psychotherapist readers if we tried to expunge all customary terminology from the text. I hope the follow-ing, brief introduction will help newcomers to the field negotiate the pages that follow.

The first idea is that of *transference*. If you were to ask me what is the single most important clinical notion in psychoanalysis, my answer would be transference. What are "transferred" into the consultation and on to the therapist are patterns of relatedness and relationship that characterize this particular patient. Often such patterns are rooted in a person's past relationships, including early relationships. In his discussion of the case of Dora (Freud, 1905e [1901]), Freud elaborated thus:

> What are transferences? They are new editions or facsimiles of the impulses and phantasies which are aroused and made conscious during the progress of the analysis; but they have this peculiarity, which is characteristic for their species, that they replace some earlier person by the person of the physi-cian. [p. 116]

We shall encounter many examples in case vignettes throughout the book.

What, then does it mean to "work" in the transference? There are two intertwined elements here. First, a therapist is seeking to identify and understand the transference—that is, this particular patient's ways of experiencing, relating to, and dealing with the therapist. Second, the therapist is trying to *interpret* what is hap-pening. This might mean no more than the therapist highlighting what the patient has said, or how the patient has communicated something by word or gesture. The aim is to bring out the meaning in what has taken place, or perhaps the fact that this has meaning, even when the specifics of what it means are not yet known. Or the therapist may suggest links among seemingly unconnected parts of a patient's story. In particular, a therapist may choose to note relations among a patient's current behaviour in the setting of the consultation, his or her reports of childhood experiences, and/or his or her descriptions of current relationships and other aspects of everyday life.

I have stated that the two elements of recognizing the transfer-ence on the one hand, and giving interpretations of the transfer-ence on the other, are intertwined. One reason this is so is that an important source of understanding the current relationship is for the therapist to register how a patient responds to the therapist's interventions. These responses are a deeply significant part of the transference.

A related concept is that of the *countertransference*. Initially, this term referred to a therapist's own transference patterns. These were (and are) considered to have the potential to distort a therapist's perception and judgement, and impede treatment. Subsequently, the weight of meaning has shifted. The term countertransference still refers to how a therapist thinks and feels in relation to a patient, but now the emphasis is upon that aspect of the therapist's experience that reflects something generated in response to this particular patient in this particular setting. The idea is that if a therapist can register and think about his or her own responses to the patient, then this may yield important insights into what the patient is bringing and doing to configure the interaction, and the respective roles of therapist and patient, in a certain way. In other words, the countertransference may be one of the most sensitive indicators of the transference.

Then there is the notion of the internal world of so-called *object relations*. I shall discuss this concept in chapter 7, when reviewing Freud's classic paper, "Mourning and Melancholia" (1917e [1915]). The central idea is that the mind is shaped by phantasies that comprise different figures who exist in relation with one another, rather as a theatre production comprises *dramatis personae* who live out their different parts. For many intents and purposes, the word "object" can be translated into "person". The source of the word "object" lies in Freud's notion that drives are directed towards the objects of those drives. The reason that the term remains in use is that the word "person" does not work when someone is relating to others as something less than, but related to, a person—for instance as a source of nourishment or a place into which feelings can be evacuated. If one is the target of such "part-object" relatedness, one feels as if one is being used in a not-fully-personal way. The phrase "object relations" is used to refer to what happens inside a person's mind, but sometimes it is applied, rather loosely, to what happens between the person and others, including the therapist.

In Kleinian thinking, special importance is attached to two contrasting object relational frames of mind—namely, the paranoid-schizoid and depressive positions. In the paranoid-schizoid position, an individual is in the world of nightmare or fairy-tale, where other people are experienced either as wonderful or as persecuting and malign—the guardian angel or wicked witch—and the person's predominant anxieties include those to do with threats to the self by invasion, exploitation, or annihilation. In the depressive position, on the other hand, a person experiences others in a way that is more rounded and more personal. Other people are felt to have their own subjective perspectives and value, and they attract ambivalent feelings of love and hate. Here, the emotional field is coloured by concern and compassion, both towards and from other people, and anxieties often centre on harming or losing much-needed people on whom one depends. Although the depressive position is seen as a developmental achievement that depends on a very young child's experience of sufficiently sensitive and containing care from at least one other person, most of us have the potential to find ourselves in each of the two positions, depending on circumstances as well as on our individual developmental histories. From moment to moment within a consultation, a person's emotional stance may shift from one position to the other.

Finally, there are the notions of *identification* and *projective identification*. To identify with someone is to assimilate within oneself what one perceives to be another person's attitudes or characteristics. A simple example is a boy who identifies with his father (like my father before me, I became a pipe-smoking psychotherapist). Projective identification is rather different. It concerns an unconscious action of ridding oneself of—and often, communicating—feelings by locating them in someone else. For instance, a narcissistic person can locate the more dependent and vulnerable aspects of him/herself in others, so that *they* become the dependent and potentially abandoned ones. The meaning of "locate" is complex here, because the feelings in question still belong to the patient, even if the therapist feels in accordance with what the patient might or should be feeling for him/herself. Projective identification is one powerful and important means by which a patient can establish and orchestrate the transference–countertransference dance.

FRAMEWORKS FOR PRACTICE

What is one "assessing" when conducting consultations in psychoanalytic psychotherapy? What is contentious about how one should conduct such interviews? What difference does context make to the process? Come to that, why assess patients at all? Part II is concerned with questions such as these.

CHAPTER 2

Assessing for psychoanalytic psychotherapy: a historical perspective

Ruth Berkowitz

> I must however make it clear that what I am asserting is that
> this technique is the only one suited to my individuality;
> I do not venture to deny that a physician quite differently
> constituted might find himself driven to adopt a different
> attitude to his patients and to the task before him.
>
> [Freud, 1912e, p. 111]

The idea that those seeking psychoanalytic treatment need to be carefully selected was first proposed by Freud (1904a, 1905a, 1912e, 1937c). On the basis of a meeting, variously called an assessment, a consultation, or an evaluation, the clinician assesses the prospective patient. The number of works cited in this chapter is testimony to the thought and effort that this idea has generated. Through what is now a century of deliberation, a morass of published work has been

---

This is a shortened and substantially modified version of my chapter "Assessment for Psychoanalytic Psychotherapy: An Overview of the Literature", in J. Cooper & H. Alfillé (Eds.), *Assessment in Psychotherapy* (1998, reprinted 2005). With permission from Karnac, publishers.

punctuated at intervals by review articles that seem to attempt to bring attention at least, and a little order at best, to some of the confusions and loopholes.

What seems to be an omission in most papers is an explanation of *why* an assessment should be done for a treatment such as psychoanalysis or psychoanalytic psychotherapy. Few authors express their views about the consequences of not assessing patients in this way, although it would seem that there are tacit understandings. A second omission in most papers is a definition of what constitutes psychoanalytic treatment, even though the demands and rigours of the experience must influence the rationale for assessment.

In this chapter, I address the factors that need to be considered when a patient and a therapist are deciding to embark on the process called psychoanalytic psychotherapy. Given that much of the literature concerns psychoanalysis, I shall make the simplifying assumption—which may not be entirely justified—that many of the considerations apply to psychoanalytic psychotherapy and psychoanalysis alike. The focus is on the qualities of the patient, the personality of the psychotherapist, and the patient–therapist match. I also consider various aspects of the process of assessment. References to clinical and more formal research studies are included. Each kind of investigation has particular strengths and weaknesses. Bloch's (1979) sceptical appraisal still hits uncomfortably near the mark:

> The immense volume of research in the area of assessment has yielded little of practical value and the impact of research on clinical work has been minimal. [p. 205]

Patient qualities

The early descriptions of patient qualities relevant for engagement in psychoanalytic psychotherapy provide evidence of a state of confusion that still continues to be the case. As Baker (1980) concluded, "In scanning the psychoanalytic literature it is possible to reach the conclusion that psychoanalysis is suitable for everything and nothing" (p. 355). For excellent reviews of the earlier literature, the reader is referred to Tyson and Sandler (1971) and Erie and Goldberg (1979). From the earliest times, Freud (1904a, 1905a, 1912e, 1937c), in outlining his views of the symptoms, qualifications, indications, and contraindications of the prospective psychoanalytic patient, considered it important to look beyond the diagnosis or illness to the whole personality. Chronic cases of psychoneuroses without very violent or dangerous symptoms were considered the most favourable for psychoanalysis. Freud excluded psychoses, states of confusion, and deeply rooted depression, although at that time he held the view that, given suitable changes in the method, this contraindication could be overcome and that there could be a psychotherapy of the psychoses. In looking beyond the patient's illness to the whole personality, he emphasized intelligence, ethical development (i.e., persons of a reliable character), and those under 50 years of age. Over the age of 50, according to Freud, the mass of psychic material was no longer manageable, the time required for recovery too long, and the ability to undo the psychic processes beginning to grow weaker. In addition, patients should come to treatment because of their own suffering, not because of the authority of a relative. The character disorders were excluded at this stage, and, as Tyson and Sandler (1971) point out, it was only when Wilhelm Reich published his book on this topic in 1933 that the diagnostic group appeared in lists.

Authors such as Fenichel (1945) and Glover (1954), while offering lists of diagnoses, stressed that the personality behind a diagnosis should be considered, and that diagnosis alone was an inadequate guide to patient selection. Glover (1954) also took into account the developmental stage of early life in which the illness could be seen as rooted. He based his diagnoses on a developmental approach— for example, with anxiety hysteria having its origins between 4 and 5 years of age, obsessional neurosis between 3 and 4, and psychoses in the first three years of life. In an "accessible" category, Glover included such diagnoses as anxiety hysteria, conversion hysteria, and mixed neuroses. The deciding feature was that the predominant anxiety should arise from the later infantile genital phases of development. The use of the term "accessible" (although not new, as it was used by Freud) added a further dimension to the issue of assessment. Glover's use of the term was linked to the transference: the earlier the fixation points, the more tenuous is the positive transference bond and the less accessible is the patient to the opening-up process.

The idea that diagnosis on its own can be misleading was highlighted in a paper by Zetzel (1968), "The So-called Good Hysteric", in which she described four categories of patients who had been diagnosed as hysterics. These patients were differentiated from one another on a variety of criteria—developmental, defences, work and academic achievements, and birth order in family of origin. Most interestingly, she marked out those whom she termed the "so-called good hysteric", whose unsuitability for psychoanalytic treatment became evident only as treatment progressed, in terms of the following criteria: absence of significant separation from parents in the first four years of life; serious pathology in one or more parents, often associated with a broken or unhappy marriage; serious and prolonged physical illness in childhood; a continuing hostile dependent relationship with the mother, who is seen as devaluing and rejecting or is devalued; and, finally, an absence of meaningful and sustained object relations with either sex. Zetzel was perhaps one of the first to consider the role of the patient's object (personal) relations—not only early, but also current—as being important.

In a paper entitled "Problems in the Selection of Patients for Psychoanalysis", Tyson and Sandler (1971) avoided the pitfalls into which others had fallen when employing terms such as indications/contraindications, suitability, accessibility, and analysability. "Indications", they suggested, were "signs and symptoms", whereas suitability had more to do with the qualities and capacities of the patient. Assessment for treatment, according to these authors, depends more on criteria of suitability than on indications. They suggested that instead of talking about the suitability of the patient for the treatment, it is more appropriate to talk about the suitability of the treatment for the person. Tyson and Sandler (1971) understood accessibility in terms of the various components necessary for an adequate treatment alliance. In particular, they emphasized a person's capacity to tolerate a certain amount of frustration, to regard him/herself as one might regard another, to experience a degree of basic trust, and to identify with the aims of treatment.

Tyson and Sandler's (1971) paper, then, usefully reviewed the literature up to 1971, taking as a framework Freud's criteria of suitability:

1. The upper age limit set at 50 by Freud was increased by subsequent writers, notably Abraham (1919), who suggested that the age of the neurosis was more important than the age of the patient. Tyson and Sandler themselves concluded that "an assessment must take into account the changes due to age in the individual patient rather than the simple factor of age itself" (p. 220).

2. Intelligence or education might be considered in terms of whether or not the patient can develop a treatment alliance and a sufficient degree of insight.

3. As regards moral and ethical considerations, Tyson and Sandler, while quoting authors such as Jones (1920) and Bibring (1937), suggested (as did Fenichel, 1945) that a patient with one type of moral problem may be acceptable to one analyst and not to another. In such a case, the analyst should not try to set aside feelings but, rather, should refer the patient elsewhere.

4. Freud (1905a) had suggested that the patient should be motivated by the fact that he suffers from his symptoms. Later, Freud (1926d [1925]) identified secondary gain—that is, drawing advantage from symptoms—to be a complicating factor. Tyson and Sandler warned that some patients may have so much to lose in the form of secondary gain that analysis may not be a viable proposition.

Tyson and Sandler (1971) wryly concluded that "It would seem that we may be in the paradoxical position of finding that the patient who is ideally suited for analysis, is in no need of it!" (p. 227).

More recent approaches

Considerable clinical and research effort has been devoted to the search for patient qualities that are relevant for decisions about psychotherapeutic treatment. Waldhorn's (1960) dictum "sick enough to need it and healthy enough to stand it" contains more than a little wisdom, especially in its reference to a person's strengths. In a similar vein, Greenson (1967) suggested that a diagnosis may not tell us much about the healthy resources of the patient. Even perversions and borderline diagnoses have "varying degrees of healthy resources. Yet it is their supply of assets, not the pathology which may be the decisive factor" (p. 53). Greenson went on to suggest that what needs to be assessed is the patient's endowment with regard to the specific demands of psychoanalytic therapy.

Therefore, the search has continued for qualities that reflect both the pathological and the healthy aspects of the patient. Here it is salutary to observe that in their review of the literature, Bachrach and Leaff (1978) listed 390 individual but widely overlapping items that different authors have considered important in predicting analysability. With regard to the categories employed below, it is important to note that these have been generated by a variety of assessment methods, ranging from clinical interviews with an emphasis on life history, diagnostic psychological testing (Kernberg et al., 1972), decisions by committee, and studies of treatment outcome. Drawing on the extensive review of the literature by Bachrach and Leaff (1978), one might consider patient characteristics under the following headings:

1.   Adequacy of general personality functioning
2.   Psychological-mindedness
3.   Ego strength, motivation, and affect
4.   Object relations.

Adequacy of general personality functioning

Relevant factors include adaptive functioning, severity of illness, severity of symptoms, diagnosis, ego strength, reality testing, sublimatory potential, adaptive regression, defence, thinking, intellectual abilities, and capacity for verbalization. Some have highlighted the need for a high degree of honesty and integrity (Greenson, 1967); to be reliable (Klauber, 1971); and to have moral awareness and integrity (Coltart, 1987). Others (e.g., Huxster, Lower, & Escott, 1975; Stone, 1954; Zetzel, 1965) have pointed to the relevance of a person's low self-esteem, harsh superego, need for punishment, self-deprecation, and a history of negative reactions to successful achievements. Klauber (1971) expressed wariness about patients with psychosomatic complaints without other conflicts, those with hypochondriasis, and those who are making their own or someone else's life impossible.

Subsequent to this, Coltart (1987) pointed out that there have been advances in the theory and treatment of severe narcissistic disorders. She expressed reservations about the prospects for cases of depression with affective flatness and projective mechanisms that might point to a concealed narcissistic disorder, as well as about the presence of "false-self" pathology. However, Coltart also wrote that other conditions formerly regarded as not suitable for psychoanalytic treatment—for example, psychosomatic states, delinquency, psychotic signs or behaviour trends, too-long periods of previous treatment, very high levels of anxiety and tension, or a patient older than the therapist—may all be dealt with by psychoanalytic therapists who have an interest in, and extended knowledge of, a particular area of disturbance. The implication is that psychoanalytic psychotherapy may be a treatment of choice for a far greater range of patients than formerly thought.

Psychological-mindedness

A related category is that of *psychological-mindedness*. This has been characterized in various ways by different authors: a capacity for self-observation or self-appraisal as opposed to rationalization (Stone, 1954); the ability to establish distance from one's own emotional experience (Namnum, 1968); the ability to carry out ego functions that are in contradiction to one another, such as in free association, and to regress in thinking but also rebound from regression in relation to the analyst; the ability to have resilient and flexible ego functions (Greenson, 1967); the ability to think in psychological terms; and, finally, the ability to see connections between events and personal feelings (Tyson & Sandler, 1971). On the other hand, Sashin, Eldred, and Van Amerongen (1975), in an attempt to rate the usefulness of specific factors in the reports of individual evaluation interviews on patients accepted for supervised psychoanalytic treatment, found that there was very little inter-rater reliability on the criterion of psychological-mindedness.

On the basis of clinical interviews, Coltart (1987) expressed the view that if someone shows a lively curiosity and a genuine concern about internal reality, then this bodes well for treatment:

> if he can make a tenuous link between the idea of relief from psychic pain and an increase in self knowledge, and then shows some real pleasure in finding out some tiny thing about himself in the initial interview, this is one of the best criteria for the analytical approach. [Coltart, 1987, p. 23]

Ego strength, motivation, and affect

Another oft-cited notion is that of ego strength. According to Kernberg (Kernberg et al., 1972), good initial ego strength is correlated with degree of improvement. On the other hand, Sashin, Eldred, and Van Amerongen (1975), in the study mentioned above, found low inter-rater reliability on the criterion of ego strength. Baker (1980) approached the question of ego strength from the perspective of defences, suggesting that the widespread deployment of primitive defences is an ominous sign, the more so when they appear to be in the service of ego stability. He goes on to say that the successful operation of such defences can mask ominous signs of ego weakness, such as in the capacity to tolerate anxiety and the precarious mastery of impulse control.

Although some clinicians have regarded motivation as a significant variable in the selection of patients (Aarons, 1962; Greenson, 1967; Knapp, Levin, McCarter, Wetment, & Zetzel, 1960; Sashin, Eldred, & Van Amerongen, 1975; Tyson & Sandler, 1971), Kernberg (Kernberg et al., 1972) did not regard it as playing an important role. Similarly, Kantrowitz (1987) considered that not only was this difficult to evaluate, but also it did not predict outcome.

A number of authors have referred to a person's organization of affect. Stone (1954) emphasized a capacity for patience and deliberate tolerance of unavoidable suffering. Zetzel (1965) wrote of the capacity to withstand anxiety and depression, Kernberg (Kernberg et al., 1972) of high initial anxiety tolerance, and Tyson and Sandler (1971) of a capacity to tolerate and recognize affect. Once again, Kantrowitz et al. (1989) suggested that affect availability and tolerance are not predictive of successful outcome.

Object relations

Then we come to the factor of "object relations", which encompasses much of what has gone before. Traditionally, object relations have been viewed mainly in terms of a person's earliest relationships, although some authors such as Zetzel (1968) and Sashin, Eldred, and Van Amerongen (1975) drew attention to current relationships of the patient as well. The topic would include considerations of narcissism, tolerance of separation, and capacity for transference and working alliance. Early object relationships were emphasized by Stone (1954), who took a longitudinal history and considered the character and pattern of relationships with people. Aarons (1962) suggested that a high quality of a person's earliest object relationships may provide a reliable basis for an assessment of analysability (see also Knapp et al., 1960; Namnum, 1968; Zetzel, 1965; however, for an opposing view, see Kantrowitz et al., 1989). Sashin, Eldred, and Van Amerongen (1975) noted that patients who left their analysis prematurely (within six months or even after three years) tended to have a poor relationship with the same-sex parent.

In recent times, a person's reaction to the assessment process, including his or her transference to the assessor, have been given increasing importance. Klauber (1971) suggested that the quality of the rapport formed as a result of glimpsing the emotional and intellectual process of psychotherapy will enable the patient and the consultant to judge whether the patient can make further use of the experience. In Klauber's view, the assessment is

> based on a complex assessment of defences and motives and arrives at a richer and profoundly relevant picture of the personality extending far back into the history of the patient. The most important thing is for it to take account of the intensity

of the compulsions to repeat old patterns of behaviour, both within and outside the analysis. [pp. 150–151]

Hinshelwood (1995), too, has considered how, in addition to infantile object relationships and the current life situation, one needs to take into account the relationship to the assessor. Garelick (1994) delineated the historical movement away from diagnosis and towards the nature of the relationship and transactions between patient and assessor. In this regard, Ogden (1989) sees the patient's history as being conveyed unconsciously in the form of transference–countertransference experience. This, he says, is the patient's living past. It comprises the set of object relations established in infancy and early childhood which has come to constitute the structure of the patient's mind both as the content and context of his or her psychological life.

Overview of patient characteristics

Before coming to a summary of supposedly important patient characteristics, it is worth considering demographic and other "external" factors. Age has been discussed above. Other factors such as occupation and life situation were considered relevant by Stone (1954). However, Bloch (1979) suggested that age, sex, marital status, educational achievement, and socioeconomic status were not of prognostic relevance. Huxster, Lower, and Escott (1975) noted that achievements in school and work were important, as did Coltart (1987), who suggested that the person who fails at everything will fail at analysis as well. Greenson (1967) suggested that prospective patients should not be in the midst of a life crisis.

In taking an overview, then, Bachrach and Leaff (1978) provided the following inventory of qualities of character relevant for psychoanalytic therapy:

Taken together these studies suggest that persons most suitable for classical psychoanalysis are those whose functioning is generally adequate; they have good ego strength, effective reality testing and sublimatory channels, and are able to cope flexibly, communicate verbally, think in secondary-process terms, and regress in the service of the ego with sufficient intellect to negotiate the tasks of psychoanalysis; their symptoms are not predominantly severe, and their diagnoses fall within a "neurotic" spectrum. Such persons are able to form a transference neurosis and therapeutic alliance, are relatively free of narcissistic pathology, have good object relations with friends, parents, and spouses, and have been able to tolerate early separations and deprivations without impairment of object constancy; they are, therefore, able to experience genuine triangular conflict. They are motivated for self-understanding, change, and to relieve personal suffering. They are persons with good tolerance for anxiety, depression, frustration, and suffering and are able to experience surges of feeling without loss of impulse control or disruption of secondary process mooring of thought. Their character attitudes and traits are well-suited to the psychoanalytic work, i.e. psychological mindedness. Superego is integrated and tolerant. They are mainly in their late twenties or early thirties and have not experienced past psychotherapeutic failure or difficulties. Of all these qualities, those relating to ego strength and object relations are most important. [pp. 885–886]

The above quotation gives what could be thought of as the definitive catalogue of characteristics of the ideal patient. However, it is worth citing the conclusions drawn by Knapp et al. (1960) from a review of 100 supervised cases:

Certainly our work suggests the impossibility of treating patients as an aggregate of unrelated and separate qualities and the difficulty, not to say impossibility, of carrying out most studies of this kind by evaluation of patients alone. The attributes and experience of the analyst, the establishment of the analytic situation, and finally, the development and resolution of the transference neurosis must all be taken into consideration. [p. 476]

Perhaps most telling of all is the comment by Bachrach and Leaff (1978) that the majority of studies fail to indicate the evidence for their conclusions, the data upon which they are based, the populations referred to, selection biases, and, in general, the extent to which one investigation may truly replicate another. As the work of Kantrowitz et al. (1989) indicates, it is questionable whether there is good agreement about the meaning of terms used. It would appear that there is much to discover. It is probably still true to say, as Bachrach and Leaff (1978) suggest, that the quantitative findings are superficial and those that are clinical are limited from a methodological point of view.

The personality of the therapist and the patient–therapist match

Freud (1905a) himself acknowledged the role of the analyst's personality in the analysis:

> It is not a modern dictum but an old saying of physicians that these diseases are not cured by the drug but by the physician, that is, by the personality of the physician, inasmuch as through it he exerts a mental influence. [p. 259]

Yet as Thompson (1938) observed:

> If one knew practical psychoanalytic experience only from the papers printed, one might be tempted to assume that the analyst as a personality in reality does not exist, that he never says anything, that he never leaves the impress of his opinion on the patient in any way, that he never makes any mistakes, that in short, he is not human but a fountain of completely detached wisdom in no way affected personally by anything which goes on. [p. 205]

This question of the personality of the analyst was considered by Stone (1954), who suggested that the analyst needs to know his own capacities (intellectual and emotional), special predilections, interests, and emotional textures, since "he may profoundly influence prognosis, and thus—in a tangible way—the indications" (p. 592). In the same journal issue, Anna Freud (1954) wrote what she considered were "technically subversive thoughts" (p. 619):

> But—and this seems important to me—so far as the patient has a healthy part of his personality, his real relationship to the analyst is never wholly submerged. With due respect for the necessary strictest handling and interpretation of the transference, I still

feel that we should leave room somewhere for the realization that analyst and patient are also two real people, of equal adult status, in a real personal relationship to each other. I wonder whether our—at times complete—neglect of this side of the matter is not responsible for some of the hostile reactions which we get from our patients and which we are apt to ascribe to "true transference" only. [pp. 618–619]

Frank (1956), in writing about what he described as the "standard technique", made the point that in his opinion psychoanalysis is a "subjective, solipsistic science, and I do not think we can shun our personalities in discussing technical matters" (p. 282). In a similar way, Knapp et al. (1960) emphasized the importance of recognizing the attributes and experience of the analyst. In 1968, Waldhorn, writing on the "lessons from the second analysis", suggested that, in those cases which by all reasonable evaluations appear suitable for analysis but prove to be incompletely or unsatisfactorily analysed,

the analyst's technical and theoretical limitations are implicated in most instances. Failure to understand the dynamics of the patient's problems or confusion about the course and sequence of the development of the analysis predispose to anxiety and errors in technique of many sorts. [p. 360]

Limentani (1972) takes a rounded view of the situation:

On the basis of my own experience and that derived from observation of supervised analyses and verbal reports from senior colleagues, I have come to recognize that many unsatisfactory outcomes are often due to a combination of factors arising from both analyst *and* patient [p. 71]

There is, however, at least one dissident voice in this—that of Kernberg (Kernberg et al., 1972), who holds the view that the skill and personality of the analyst is greatly overridden by patient factors.

Then there is the question of the therapist–patient match, a matter stressed by Waldhorn (1968), Liberman (1968), and Bachrach, Weber, and Solomon (1985). Thompson (1938) suggested that analysts ought to consider their specific liabilities and thereby learn from experience the type of case with whom they do and do not have success. Sending them elsewhere could save patients' time and possible discouragement. Pollock (1960) regarded it as an accepted fact that familiarity with a particular cultural background will permit the analyst to appreciate certain value systems, customs, and attitudes: "Without such appreciations by the analyst, things might be misunderstood or thought of as having undue pathological significance" (p. 365). In addition, he urges the therapist to pay respect when patients express strong views about the therapist's attributes. Klauber (1971) noted one possible repercussion for analysis:

> . . . an underlying conflict of value systems between patient and analyst may cause a permanent discontent which the patient is unable to articulate and which may force him to make painful psychic adjustments that can only gradually be thrown off after the analysis is ended. [p. 142)

The assessment process

Among important features of the assessment process are the nature of a referral, how the assessment is conducted, whether one or more meetings are involved, and the question of referring on to another therapist.

It may be unpromising when a patient seems to attend *merely* because he or she was referred by a professional or relative. Freud (1904a) saw it as a contraindication if a patient submitted to seeking treatment because of a relative's authority. Aarons (1962) took a different view, suggesting that the fact that a patient had come to the assessment was sufficient motivation. Pollock (1960) wrote a comprehensive paper entitled "The Role and Responsibilities of the Psychoanalytic Consultant", in which he covered many aspects of the assessment process. Pollock emphasized how details of the referral may yield important clues as to the patient's motivation, anxiety level, and resistance patterns, as well as fantasies, expectations, and goals. Along the same lines nearly thirty years later, Garelick (1994) made very similar points about the importance of attending to the context of the referral, the nature of the referral pattern, and the system from which the patient has been referred. Hinshelwood (1995) added another perspective, suggesting that object relationships in the form of transference and countertransference may often be discerned before the interview in the manner of the referral itself:

> Thus, the referral is often made on the basis of the referrer's unconscious awareness of a specific relationship. It is a kind of "acting out" on the part of the referrer who is caught up unconsciously in one of these object relationships I have been describing. This is not to the discredit of the referrer, as the awareness of these kinds of relationship is not his field of work and expertise. It is ours. But it is an added clue for us to the patient's core object relationships. [p. 163]

The conduct of assessment consultations remains a focus of controversy. Earlier writers such as Stone (1954), Waldhorn (1960), and Zetzel (1965) tended to take a longitudinal history. Garelick (1994) suggested that one of the important and, perhaps, contentious issues is the activity of the assessor who actively seeks out information as opposed to using a technique of free association and allowing the material to unfold gradually. Schubart (1989) and Shapiro (1984) recommended using an associative procedure and giving evenly suspended attention from the start, rather than extracting information.

Klauber (1971) and Coltart (1987) seemed to adopt an intermediate position. Klauber's (1971) view was that in the consultation or assessment meeting, the therapist's role is more an advisory one, directed to the functioning ego of the patient. An important decision needs to be made, with powers of judgement in operation. Coltart (1987) wrote of the consultation as follows:

> This may involve some questioning, some interpretation, some link making comments, sympathy expressed only in your whole attitude of extremely attentive listening, and some concise summarizing of your own views towards the end of the interview. [p. 26]

Ogden (1989) tried to give the patient a sense of what it means to be in analysis. He did not favour taking a history, since his view was that

> a patient's history is not a static entity that is gradually unearthed; rather, it is an aspect of the patient's conscious and

unconscious conception of himself that is in a continual state of evolution and flux. [p. 191]

Garelick (1994) provided a detailed account of his assessment technique, giving the patient an analytic type of experience, taking up issues in the here-and-now, monitoring the reaction of the patient, and identifying his own countertransference. He advocated not taking a history initially, although he might do so to relieve anxiety. The history-taking would serve to make links revealing the pattern of the patient's interpersonal relationships, separation problems, and a compulsion to repeat. He regarded this as potentially educational for the patient, conveying some understanding that the past links up with the present. Hinshelwood's view (1995) was that assessments for psychoanalytic psychotherapy should be no less psychodynamic than psychotherapy itself, and he valued making interpretations, even transference interpretations, for two reasons: first, the patient's response gives an idea of suitability and psychological-mindedness; second, it is a good preparation because it gives a taste of psychotherapy.

Should assessment consultations be extended over several sessions? Pollock (1960) was opposed to extended interviews, as he said that this interfered with the transference. Coltart (1987) appeared to conduct single diagnostic interviews, while Garelick (1994) favoured extended assessments for the following reasons: the assessor can have a more analytic stance, the patient can have more of an experience of what psychotherapy is going to be like, and the patient is likely to be more involved in the decision-making process. While there is an anxiety expressed by some that a strong transference will develop, Garelick believed that it works towards facilitating a working alliance with the next therapist, and it enables the assessor to metabolize, process, and verbalize primitive communications.

If assessing a patient's problems and appropriateness for psychoanalytic therapy depends on the therapist and the match between patient and therapist, then it should be important to consider the option of referring on to someone else. Coltart (1987) tried to match the patient with a therapist, being aware of colleagues' capabilities and special talents. She believed that some therapists have gifts for some sorts of patients and others for others.

Pollock (1960) noted there may be occasions when the relationship between the assessor and the prospective therapist can stir up performance anxieties in the therapist. He also pointed out that information should be given to a prospective psychotherapist in such a way that the latter is free of a sense of loyalty and obligation.

Conclusions

To make a recommendation for psychoanalytic psychotherapy is a serious and at times risky decision. It is serious for the patient, because of the investment of time and money, as well as carrying the potential for difficult and painful experiences. At worst, it can be a damaging experience. This might especially be the case for very deprived patients, or those unable to bear the frustrations of the analytic setting, and there may be untoward effects when fragile defences are dismantled. It is also an investment on the part of the therapist. To conduct a psychotherapy where little progress is made, or which is an experience too difficult to bear and can become interminable, should also be avoided.

At some level, an assessment is a predictive exercise. Early on, it had seemed wise to base prediction on those factors that were most easily assessed—in particular, patient qualities. Lists of these qualities extended into hundreds, and this merely highlighted how the personality behind a diagnosis is very important. Both the unhealthy and healthy aspects of a person need consideration. The conclusion that object/personal relations and ego strength are among the most important factors makes sense in terms of the analytic task that the patient faces. After all, psychoanalytic psychotherapy entails forming and sustaining a transference relationship. Such a relationship will have qualities of earlier relationships. And the capacity to manage and reflect on what transpires in psychotherapy depends on the ego strength of the patient.

It would be easy to overlook changes in the way in which the assessment consultations are conducted. Today, there is greater emphasis on the transference and countertransference, and giving the patient a sense of what is to come in the analytic experience. This is both an advance and a reflection of the changes in psychoanalytic thinking: the patient is an active participant in the assessment just as he or she is in an analysis, being one part of a dyad rather than the passive recipient of a recommendation or interpretation.

It is also more widely recognized that the course of psychoanalytic psychotherapy can be affected by the personality of the therapist, as well as the match between patient and therapist. There are particular considerations in a training experience that may influence the course of a psychotherapy, such as the nature of the referral and the supervisory experience (Epstein, 1990). While assessors may try to select and match, there are few satisfactory ways of evaluating these factors except in a post hoc manner.

These are, of course, generalizations based on clinical and (modest) research evidence. Clinical papers may struggle with definitions and sources of bias, whereas research papers, in an attempt at rigour and clarity, may filter out meaning. The way in which this review chapter has been structured, singling out aspects of the assessment procedure for consideration, mirrors problems in this field. The ingredients can be taken out and examined if not measured, but in the final analysis any assessment consultation involves a combination of all the factors discussed, put together in a particular way by a particular assessor—to articulate that is an impossible task. At the end of the day, a therapist also needs to draw on intuition, not to mention his or her own unconscious processes.

CHAPTER 3

Why assess? Psychoanalytic assessment in the National Health Service

Jane Milton

B efore the question of the title, "why assess?", there is another question—what *is* a so-called "assessment"?—and what do we as psychoanalytic psychotherapists in the NHS *mean* by assessment?

It is important not to start off with too narrow a focus. When I am referred a patient for an NHS assessment, I try to keep in mind that I am not just doing something called "assessment for psychotherapy", especially not just "assessment for psychotherapy here in my institution". Rather, I am conducting a psychoanalytically informed interview with someone so that, in a limited time, I can get a picture of the person's inner world and the way it functions and understand the nature of the distress with which the person presents. This will help me to comment to the patient and the referrer about a number of things, only one of which is the patient's so-called suitability for psychotherapy.

This is an amended version of Milton, J. (1997), "Why Assess? Psychoanalytical Assessment in the NHS". *Psychoanalytic Psychotherapy*, 11: 47–58, appearing by permission of the publisher (Taylor & Francis Ltd, http://www.informaworld.com).

Simultaneously, the patient will have the opportunity to assess the nature of the psychoanalytic process, and think about whether or not this is an investigation with which he or she wishes to proceed. The referrer, the patient, and often, it has to be said, the institution where one works may well see the whole enterprise as a sort of test that the patient will pass or fail and either be accepted or rejected for the treatment on offer. If one thinks of assessment in too narrow a way, it can cause one to adopt a style of communication with the referrer that is unsatisfactory. The message may seem to be: "Your patient wasn't appropriate for referral and is not good enough for this excellent but rare and precious treatment."

To many, the word "assessment" itself may imply a value judgment, or an attempt to place someone along a scale of suitability. The *Concise Oxford Dictionary* states that, indeed, "to assess" means to estimate the size, quality, or value of something, and that an assessor is someone who estimates the value of property for tax purposes. However, an alternative definition of an assessor, fortunately, is a person *called in to advise on technical matters*. I think this latter definition captures the role much more adequately. Often the term "consultation" may be more appropriate.

The psychoanalytic assessment is one of the most important and interesting aspects of our work. We are very privileged as psychoanalytic psychotherapists to be given detailed and intimate access to the mind of a hitherto total stranger. For the patient, it is often a completely new experience that may be disturbing, exhilarating, relieving, or intensely intrusive and frightening or enraging. Learning about assessments and developing one's own method and style of assessing is a vital part of psychotherapy training in the public sector. Assessment styles and philosophies encountered during a trainee's apprenticeship phase of NHS work, when the trainee is trying to develop his or her own approach, may differ considerably. To explore this, I shall caricature two very different styles of assessment that have importantly differing implications.

Dr A conducts an assessment interview in a way that approximates at first to an ordinary analytic session. The patient is greeted courteously but gravely and is subjected from the outset to an intense scrutiny. Dr A gives the minimum of instruction and eschews measures that might be described as "putting the patient at ease". The patient is invited by a brief word to begin wherever the person wishes and is then given absolute attention. However, the patient is not given customary social responses—for example, smiles or attempts to "chat". Dr A works hard, and in a very detailed way, studying transference and countertransference and interprets what is happening in order to deepen understanding. Often very rapid, perhaps unnervingly rapid, access is gained to the patient's areas of vulnerability—for example, depression or paranoia, or sadomasochistic patterns of relating. These can then be examined in detail. Later, Dr A may undertake some more direct questioning to fill in important gaps in the emerging story. The way the story is told will be studied, and the patient may be invited to think about why certain topics (e.g., say, his or her relationship with the father) had not emerged before. The use of a pre-interview questionnaire helps with this sort of assessment, as important background information is already available.

Dr B, on the other hand, greets the patient in a more conventional way and tends to respond to some of the social cues when the patient seems to be seeking him to give reassurance that he is a benign figure. Analytically speaking, the opportunity is not taken *directly* to explore the paranoid anxiety underlying this need for reassurance. While Dr A's strict neutrality allows for (and, in a way, prompts) disturbance to arise, Dr B feels that it is wrong, perhaps unacceptably intrusive, to expose the patient to these sorts of anxieties in an assessment. Dr B might argue that he is not going to be the therapist, and the patient may have to wait a long time for treatment. He prefers to discuss the patient's more paranoid anxieties in the "there-and-then" of recollected experience, rather than in the "here-and-now" of the lived present. Therefore, Dr B centres the interview on active history-taking, asking the patient about the details of symptoms and relationships, to supplement what is already known from the questionnaire. He is, in the main, talking *to* an observing part of the patient *about* the distressed aspects of the person's life.

Having done hundreds of such interviews myself now, experimenting with different ways, and thinking about what I am trying to do and why, I now find myself at a point on the scale joining Drs A and B, tending more towards Dr A. Although I run a greater risk of offending and upsetting patients, at least in the early part of an interview, my personal view is that I do them a better service by not responding to their social cues and, thereby, engaging more directly with their disturbance. After all, by maintaining neutrality and working in the transference, we have the opportunity to become a fresh and unexpected figure in the patient's life. This is because, in a normal social encounter, when the patient experiences someone else in terms of an unreal imagined fantasy, the other person will tend to respond automatically to the patient's unconscious cues to become such or, alternatively, bend over backwards to become a reassuringly opposite figure. The analytic assessor, by his or her hard work in resisting such pressure, remaining neutral and instead interpreting, will sometimes be revealed as a more three-dimensional and alive person to the patient and will often help the patient—for that hour or two at least—to come more alive and three-dimensional him/herself, to see things in a new way, and to be freer to think. Garelick (1994), in his comprehensive review of the subject of assessment, recommends that one assesses over at least two sessions, in order to allow time for an initial unstructured approach followed by a phase of information gathering. Increasingly, this is my own practice.

Thus, when I talk about my model of assessment, or analytic consultation, which I know I share with many, I am talking about an *invasive* procedure or investigation. In medical terms, "invasive" is a term describing investigations that mean breaking into the body in some physical way. So listening to the chest or taking an X-ray are not very invasive, but taking a sample of fluid from a body cavity, or putting a tube into the lung, or opening up the abdomen to examine how far a cancer has spread *are* invasive. Invasive procedures should not be done unless there is a good reason and there is no other option (such as a sophisticated form of scan) available. They tend not only to be painful, frightening, and inconvenient for the patient, but they also involve bodily disruption and some danger. So we have to have a good reason to do a psychological investigation that tends to break in to the inner world, piercing defences, and potentially causing mental pain and upset. This is especially the case when we have before us a patient who is not in active pain and distress *at that moment*. It might also be mentioned that just as we would not wish an inexperienced clinician to perform a dangerous and invasive medical investigation on us, so too we would want to regard psychoanalytic assessment as a relatively advanced procedure not to be practised by the novice without careful supervision and training.

Considerations of invasiveness may be less fraught when a patient comes in a state of obvious pain and anxiety such that interpretation is needed almost as an emergency procedure, bringing visible relief. This is often not the case, however, in a standard psychotherapy service (as opposed to a crisis intervention service), as, by the time the appointment arrives, the crisis has often abated and some sort of defence is back in place. However, one tends to find that there are two broad categories of person in this respect: (1) the person whose complaint and *presentation* is an anxious, actively distressed one, or where the distress is only just below the surface and is easily reached; and (2) the person whose presentation is in the form of the defence itself, possibly with *reported* episodes of breakthrough of anxiety, such as panic attacks, but presenting for assessment in the thoroughly defended, cut-off state. It is the latter category of person, rather than the former, who will dislike the opening-up procedure of the interview most and will face us with a dilemma. On the one hand, we are being asked not to intrude. On the other hand, we might be betraying the patient and colluding with defences by not being invasive enough.

So, having set the scene a little by saying what I mean by "assessment", I will ask the question of my title—*why* assess? Why do we perform this invasive investigative procedure on people? To start with, when would we decide not to proceed with an assessment consultation? Would there be circumstances in which we thought from the referral that it was likely to do more harm than good? I think this is bound to be so.

Case vignette: Mr C

A GP asked our clinic to assess Mr C for psychotherapy. In the referral letter, it was mentioned that Mr C had received assessments in a number of places, including in the catchment-area mental health team and the local psychology service and by a private counselling organization. He had been extremely dissatisfied with the care he had received so far and had lodged a complaint about the local psychiatrist with the health authority. He had also sent a series of angry letters to the head of the counselling service, complaining that the person he had seen had stared at him in an aggressive way, and he demanded another interview with someone more senior, who would "give him more feedback". The referrer felt, she said, that the "very special skills" of the Tavistock Clinic were needed to contain such a difficult patient, and that he needed long-term individual psychotherapy. We were asked if we could see him as an emergency, as he was causing considerable anxiety to his family and to the practice, which he visited almost daily in an anxious and angry state.

In my view, to offer this patient an assessment interview would have been provocative and unhelpful, and a reflection of omnipotence. The litigious, near-psychotic, or frankly psychotic potential of this person was clearly manifest, even without a meeting. Although an interview might have revealed all sorts of interesting pathology, it would have inflamed the patient and raised false expectations. The most useful way we could help was by engaging in a detailed and thoughtful telephone consultation with the GP about management of this highly disturbing situation.

The next example concerns a patient of this sort who was offered an assessment, with potentially dangerous consequences.

Case vignette: Mr D

Mr D was referred to an outpatient psychotherapy clinic with chronic anxiety and depression; again, the urgency of the referral was stressed by the GP, who mentioned that the local psychiatrists had seen him and prescribed antidepressants, but that the patient was no better. Reference was made to a disturbed and abusive childhood, but little more detail was given. The patient was sent the standard questionnaire, with the usual request to fill in as much as possible and to get in touch if there were any difficulties.

Mr D turned up at the Clinic in an agitated state the next day, and the receptionist asked the duty medical registrar to see him. Mr D had his questionnaire with him, and he said that he was afraid to fill it in, in case the biro damaged the paper as he wrote. He had a number of other anxious preoccupations, and the on-call clinician ended up spending an hour with him, even though she had intended to spend only 10 minutes. He seemed very persecuted, but not frankly psychotic. He left in a calmer state and managed to deliver the questionnaire by hand the next day.

At this stage, the supervisor encouraged the trainee assessor to carry on and offer a formal assessment appointment. Mr D, unable to wait the two weeks for his appointment, turned up at the Clinic on two further occasions, needing to be seen by a duty person again before he would leave the building. The assessment interview itself, as might by now have been predicted, turned up copious disturbing, near-psychotic material. The patient became fragmented in the unstructured setting, so that the assessor had to modify her technique rapidly. He formed an intensely dependent, idealizing transference to her, which turned to a confused rage when it became evident to him that she was not about to offer him individual therapy herself and, indeed, was trying to talk to him about how he might feel more secure in a hospital at this point. She felt in physical danger and had to call on all her pre-analytic social-work skills in addressing the residual sane part of Mr D, and to encourage him to walk with her to the lift and then to go to the GP, to whom she spoke immediately.

These examples should not be understood as meaning that a disturbed individual who is unlikely to be offered outpatient psychotherapy should never be offered an assessment. Often something very useful is to be gained from offering a psychoanalytic interview to someone with, say, a psychotic illness in remission, or someone else in whom a dynamic formulation has to be made in order to inform management. It is important in such cases, however, to do preliminary work with the referrer and try to avoid raising unrealistic expectations.

So, why *do* we assess for psychotherapy? Why do we need to subject the patient to the sort of disturbing and intrusive psychoanalytic investigation that I have outlined? Why, after ruling out the more disturbed cases referred to above, do we not simply offer more or less everyone who asks for it a chance to engage in a therapeutic relationship, say on a first-come, first-served basis, if, as we know, rationing is inevitable? I do have some sympathy with the idea of erring on the generous side, of giving people a chance at psychotherapy, as long as they seem to want it and have been given as clear an idea as possible what it will involve. I would like to argue that it is not so much for us to say "who is suitable?" (as, in fact, that is a surprisingly hard thing to do) but, rather, to identify patients for whom psychotherapy, at least in certain settings, is contraindicated and either harmful or likely to be useless. I would like to suggest that we should observe a hierarchy of aims involved in roughly the order below. Here I am borrowing from Maslow's (1954) concept of "hierarchy of needs", where he considers the way in which, for us as human beings, basic survival needs have to come before more complex social and psychological requirements:

1.   Patient and therapist physical safety
2.   Patient mental safety
3.   Patient privacy and dignity
4.   Indicators of patient "suitability"
5.   Training needs of the therapist
6.   Economic considerations.

Before going through these points in turn, giving some illustrative clinical examples, I would stress the importance of the *context* of the assessment interview. Is the assessor working in a hospital outpatient department? Is the assessment and/or treatment to take place in the same building as acute wards or a day hospital, or in an isolated psychotherapy unit? What sort of psychotherapy is available: how long-term, how intensive, and what is the waiting list like? What other treatments are available elsewhere, in the NHS or outside?

The well-known dictum *first do no harm* has to be paramount. This means it is important to try to avoid doing something that will make the patient's situation fundamentally worse, either by the assessment itself, or by offering a particular treatment. I have already given case examples where considerations of physical safety, for both patient and therapist, suggest that we should consider not offering an interview, given the situation of a service that offers only outpatient treatment and no crisis service. Considerations of physical safety must also be taken into account when recommending the form of treatment.

Case vignette: Mr E

Mr E asked his GP to be referred for psychotherapy, as he was frightened of his uncontrolled violence. He had spent several years in prison for a violent attack on a member of a right-wing organization, during what had started as a peaceful anti-fascist demonstration. His friends included both hardened criminals with a hatred and grievance against society and others, and others with more hopeful and encouraging attitudes. This reflected a deep split within himself. He had spent most of his childhood in care, having suffered violent abuse from parents and step-parents. There had, however, been one supportive social worker with whom he had formed a strong bond. This person seemed to have helped him to retain some sense of hope and ambition to make something of his life.

In the unstructured assessment interview, Mr E quickly went white, became sweaty with fear, and felt attacked and judged by the therapist. He wanted to leave the room, but with much active interpretive help from the assessor, he managed to hang on to himself and have a conversation about what was happening. He was able to talk about his fears of violence. Towards the end of the first interview, with fear and shame, he was able to agree with the therapist's observation that there was a "fascist" part of himself who was both a protector and a vengeful aggressor.

The second meeting took place a week later, and Mr E reported high levels of anxiety over the intervening days. He had experienced impulses to violence towards himself and others, which it was only just possible for him to resist. However, he remained adamant that he wanted to explore things and try to change. He pointed out that nothing else had helped, and he felt at the end of the road. Having thought carefully about the options, the assessor decided that only a residential setting would provide enough safety for Mr E and, indeed, for the professionals working with him, who at some time would inevitably become the hated fascists in the transference.

My next point in the hierarchy concerns *mental safety*. This is relevant for the patient who had fears of harming the paper of the questionnaire with his biro. Any analytic investigation is inviting possible *breakdown*. For many, some form of "breakdown", major or minor, will be an inevitable, perhaps a necessary part of the treatment process—that is, breakdown of the defensive structure and emergence or break-*through* of the underlying grief, paranoid fear, and so on. We have to consider carefully and responsibly, for each person, what breakdown *will mean for them*—what will be its nature if and when it occurs? Will it, for example, mean a serious psychotic decompensation? And, if so, are there any structures in place to help contain this?

Some people we see will have broken down already, with the emergence of anxiety, depression, and unravelling of their everyday existence. They are often the people who will say, "I'm afraid I'm going to have a breakdown", who can often be quite helped by being told in some way or another, "Well, actually what you are describing now is your breakdown, and this could already be as bad as it will get". Others will come in a more defended state and report episodes of depression or of panic. Part of our role is to try to uncover this in psychotherapy. Healing in a new way, with the potential for development, will not, in our way of thinking, be possible until the breakdown the person is describing "out there" has occurred in some form in the context of psychotherapy itself.

We do aim, however, in outpatient treatment at least, to provide a therapeutic setting where the breakdown will be *contained* within the treatment, so that the patient will be able to continue his or her life outside. This is where I think we have to be very careful in prescribing the right treatment. If psychotherapy is to work, it is a useful rule of thumb that the worst that the patient has experienced *will occur* in the treatment at some point. Thus, a patient with a history of manic or severe depressive episodes, however apparently sane and thoughtful he or she may have appeared in the assessment interview, will be bound to break down in the context of the therapeutic relationship (perhaps precipitated by a break, for example), unless the therapy remains at a superficial, non-analytic level. If the treatment were to be without depth, we would question why we were doing it anyway.

This is another good argument, I think, for invading enough in the assessment interview to show the patient, there and then, albeit in a small way, what this breakdown of defences, and breakthrough of anxiety and disturbance, is like. On this basis, the patient can make an informed choice. It is essential for the assessor to gauge what is the minimum therapeutic setting needed to contain the inevitable breakdown, keeping the patient safe. The therapist must also feel contained enough by the setting in which he or she works, without fears about how the patient will react hampering clinical freedom.

Case vignette: Miss F

Miss F was referred with a long history of recurrent mania, for which she had spent at least half of the last five years in hospital. The ward doctor, who felt strongly that there was a part of the patient who could think and wanted to work on herself, referred her to the psychotherapy department within the same building. The assessor, after careful consideration and discussion with colleagues, agreed with the ward doctor, and she was taken on for once-weekly therapy by the psychotherapy senior registrar.

The ward and the walk-in Emergency Clinic downstairs from the psychotherapy department were informed when Ms E was starting treatment. Her disturbance quickly became focused on the therapy and the therapist, and episodes of breakdown continued intermittently as before, but now focused around transference issues. Inevitably, the impression that therapy was making her worse was created. The tolerance of the Emergency Clinic staff, in particular, who often had to deal with an angry and histrionic or very excited and disinhibited patient arriving downstairs after her sessions, was stretched to its limits. There were often mutterings about those precious psychotherapists upstairs who did not have to do the dirty work and pick up the pieces. However, it became evident over the next two years that Ms E's breakdowns were becoming more circumscribed, and shorter in duration. She had taken to asking for help as she felt herself deteriorating, instead of, as before, being brought in by police or friends in an excited, triumphant, and inaccessible state. At times, she required brief admission and close supervision during periods of depression.

Such a patient would not have been contained in an institution geared only to outpatient work. In fact, to have offered treatment in such a non-containing setting would have transgressed my first two rules about physical and mental safety.

To move on now to the third point in this hierarchy, *patient privacy and dignity*: Patients may sometimes come to us having an idea about psychotherapy being soothing, primarily giving relief from pain, consisting of question-and-answer sessions, or providing advice or education. They may have a utopian idea about what may be readily achieved in treatment. There is often a lack of knowledge among referrers and patients about the differences between different psychotherapeutic approaches. Some are partly educational in nature, so that behavioural or cognitive therapies may allow a patient to retain defences and protect his or her privacy to a much greater extent than psychodynamic treatment. Paradoxically, it may be considered, however, that the patient is being subtly infantilized far more in such pedagogic procedures than in an analytic approach.

Some patients' fragile self-esteem or fear of what is within are such that they are simply not prepared for the sacrifice of privacy involved in psychoanalytic work. I think we should be able to let such individuals make an informed choice about this by the way we work in an assessment interview. The aim is to show them a little of what the work involves, and then, if necessary, talking to them about what might be a more bearable, albeit more palliative, procedure. However, it may seem right first to try to address and challenge a resistant part of the patient, which may be trapping a more voiceless, desperate part of him or her. If we feel we have done this to the best of our ability, the choice really is then the patient's. It is a choice he or she should be allowed to make with dignity, and the door should be left open for future discussion and review.

In the same way, a patient with a serious disease who cannot face a major operation, but opts for symptomatic relief, has a right to this. Once we have given as much information as we can about the situation to the patient, in as understandable a form as possible, it is no longer our business what course is chosen. We also have a responsibility to protect the patient's dignity and help him or her to make alternative plans, rather than simply washing our hands of him or her in a smug or moralistic way. I think the many people who drop out during the assessment process, or during the early phases of psychotherapy, are often saying "No" to the painful and disturbing intrusion involved, at least at this stage in their lives and their illness. This should be respected. It is more helpful if it can be addressed openly in the interview, rather than leaving the patient angry and humiliated, or feeling a failure and with nowhere else to turn later.

Case vignette: Mrs G

Mrs G was referred by a child guidance team who had been seeing her with her little boy, who was wild and destructive, as it was felt that she needed help in her own right. The referrer in his letter called Mrs G "a charming lady" who, in addition to her difficult child, was burdened with a difficult husband as well as an intrusive and critical mother. In the assessment interview, Mrs G offered an initial charming greeting, and her attempts to engage the assessor socially were hard to resist. Then Mrs G became resentful and suspicious in the unstructured setting, and uneasy, even outraged, at the invitation to start wherever she liked. She demanded questions that she could answer, saying that she was accustomed to talk to the doctor about her little boy and that the assessor's approach was rude and unreasonable.

It seemed to the interviewer that she (the interviewer) was probably predominantly Mrs G's mother in the transference. The patient anticipated, and indeed experienced, criticism from the interviewer. unless the latter dispelled this artificially by actively presenting herself as a good, benign figure, as there was huge pressure on her to do. Attempts to explore this dynamic were largely unsuccessful and were met with incomprehension and anger. However, the assessor sensed that, beneath the surface, Mrs G was depressed and despairing. She talked to Mrs G about her mixed feelings about exposing herself, and this Mrs G could acknowledge. It seemed that for Mrs G to reveal to herself and others her own depressed and also wild, critical, or "difficult" side was at present unbearable. In the second meeting, Mrs G said that she had decided against psychotherapy and was going instead to join a support group for mothers whose children had attention deficit disorder. Her present solution to her problems was discussed and acknowledged by the assessor, who left the door open for a further consultation in the future.

To come now to *"indicators of suitability"*. We often jump too quickly, I think, to putting this at the *top* of the list of reasons for the assessment process. In this chapter, I have been trying to come at this same issue from a different angle. I would say that the patient who has got to this stage of the assessment, who we have satisfied ourselves is not in physical or mental danger from treatment, and who has not shied away from the invasion of privacy involved, has begun to look like someone who could benefit from psychotherapeutic work. I think it can be relatively easy, with experience, to get a sense of who might do well, but it is harder to say categorically that someone is *un*suitable, and would not do well, or at least harder than we might like to think.

Along with many other psychotherapists, I dislike the use of "analysability" criteria of a didactic sort, as one can become suspiciously near to accepting only responsive and rewarding people for treatment. The irrelevance prognostically, on the whole, of psychiatric diagnosis is commonly accepted, much as we realize the irrelevance of social class, ethnicity, level of education, and so on. Psychological-mindedness, or *emotional* literacy, has a separate dimension from all of these. Sometimes the most disturbed and chaotic people can have a liveliness or curiosity or strength about them that is absent in a more ostensibly sane person. It is possible also to talk about "motivation" for treatment in a way that attempts to gauge something prematurely and can even be slightly moralistic. Realistically, motivation may be something that emerges through the patient finding out by experience *in* therapy what is or is not bearable or worthwhile.

However, I do think we should, when thinking of likelihood of benefit, be attending to the question of whether this *particular* patient might be making a useful sacrifice of time and effort in taking part in the *particular* treatment that is on offer at one's institution. For example, we may judge that a very out-of-touch or markedly perverse and stuck person *may* be wasting his or her time coming to once-weekly individual sessions and may need to be told this. It may sometimes be that we would recommend more intensive treatment if possible, and options of low-fee, more intensive treatment schemes run by training organizations might be discussed. In such situations, it may be that the patient is not necessarily "unsuitable for psychotherapy", but that *we* are the ones lacking or who are failing, in not being able to provide the specialist, intensive treatment that we would recommend for this person.

We may also sometimes be recommending a group for a patient, even though he or she might strongly prefer the idea of once-weekly individual treatment, which *we* judge will just get stuck and repetitive and offer less opportunity for change. There is often a point in the interview where the treatment of choice from our point of view may not be at all what the patient had envisaged. I think one of the functions of an assessment interview should be to enable us to give an informed view to the patient and to lay out all the options available and give our opinion as to which is the most appropriate and why. This is the point at which, I think, with the less structured, reflective work of the session over, we need to become quite openly the professional who is advising and giving an opinion. This aspect of the work is vital, and something to which the patient is entitled.

My penultimate point is about *training needs*. In practice, one of the inevitable answers to the question "why assess?" is that we might need to find suitable training cases. Many of the organizations where we work have to take into account the needs of therapists training in psychotherapeutic skills. There is often a tension here, as new therapists will want patients who are accessible and who will attend regularly and not cause too much trouble. Increasingly, of course, our patients are people with severe personality disorder, and we are often working at the limits of treatability. I think that within the NHS (as distinct from non-NHS training institutions, where the situation may be rather different), we must realize that training needs—given that we are trying to train people to work in the public sector—are more integral to service needs than might at first appear. The supervisor has a vital role in helping the trainee extract something valuable from the experience of treating a great range of patients.

Economic considerations come at the end. I have included these because in terms of what is offered, the outcome of an assessment interview may depend on whether the decision has been made by the organization on pragmatic, resource-led grounds to offer mainly a short-term therapy service, or mostly group rather than individual treatment, and so on. In some patients, we know that short-term therapy is contraindicated, as it will do more harm than good. It is important for a service to acknowledge the limitations of what it offers. The worst thing, I think, may be an idealization of brief therapy, especially where it is organized and packaged and manualized in such a way as to give the institution and therapist the comfortable illusion that a complete treatment is being offered and that any failure is subtly the fault of the patient. In my view, the best kind of brief therapy is the sort where analytic principles are applied and acknowledgement is made of the incompleteness of the process and of the resulting pain, deprivation, and dissatisfaction. Paradoxically, the better containment offered by this sort of philosophy and approach to brief treatment is likely to make it suitable for a wider range of people than treatments that are ostensibly more "sewn up" by having a so-called focus that is other than a straightforward focus on the transference.

The question of *rationing* is implicit in all this, too. Extreme rationing is sadly inevitable in psychotherapy services in the UK at this time. Often we have to turn down people in great need, or offer them something that is really quite minimal, because the sort of psychotherapy they need is not available. We must be straightforward about this to ourselves, and not use the excuse that "the patient is unsuitable", when what is actually lacking is the appropriate treatment. In the assessment *and* the therapy processes, a psychotherapist must bear the tension of knowing the limitations of the service offered. The patient should never be left at the end of an assessment interview with the message "You've failed our test", but with the message, "This is what I think you could benefit from, and why", even if it is not available.

THE CONSULTATION PROCESS

The first three chapters in Part III cover the beginning, middle, and final phases of assessment interviews. The fourth takes a closer look at the process of analysing the transference. Each represents the approach of a single psychoanalytic psychotherapist—namely, myself. I hope that the discussion of underlying principles and the presentation of clinical vignettes may allow readers to judge what they see as helpful and unhelpful in a particular way of undertaking this demanding form of consultation.

CHAPTER 4

How to begin?

R. Peter Hobson

It was only slowly that I came to conduct assessment consultations in the way that I do now. As a trainee, I was more cautious in my approach—and rightly so. I considered it appropriate to put a patient at ease, perhaps to explain the point of the meeting, and to convey how I was prepared to listen sensitively and offer reassurance and encouragement if need be. I still believe that this is an appropriate stance for a beginning psychotherapist. If it introduces limitations, even difficulties, for the task of assessment, then so, too, it avoids the kind of trauma for both patient and therapist that might arise from a therapist's attempt to enact a role—that of Psychotherapist with a capital "P"—which is inhuman and inhumane. For example, to suppose that there are *sometimes* grounds for a therapist to remain silent even though a patient wants the therapist to say something is hugely different from supposing that silence is a "good thing". On the contrary, to not respond can be damaging.

Therefore, although I am happy for more experienced trainees to sit in on my assessment interviews, I am careful when allowing beginners to do so. I take this stance for two reasons. First, many individuals who are embarking on their psychotherapy training have little grasp of what the transference means. They have learnt that "transference" refers to the fact that, in the special conditions created by the psychotherapy setting, patients transfer aspects of their important relationships on to the person of the therapist. Yet this is a long way from understanding how this plays out through moment-to-moment shifts in interpersonal engagement over the course of a consultation. I can recall a relatively experienced trainee sitting in on one of my assessment consultations in which I felt there were especially clear re-enactments of the patient's past and current relationships in relation to myself as therapist. Afterwards, I asked how far the trainee felt that what he had witnessed amounted to expressions of the transference, and he looked blank. He had simply not seen what I had seen. I doubt whether in such a case a trainee learns much that is useful; instead, he or she might be unsettled and confused by the experience.

Second, and more importantly, trainees might attempt to mimic what I do before they are ready. This relates to the dangers of trainees trying to be a "Psychotherapist" and striving to do what they suppose they are meant to be doing. Any trainee—indeed, any therapist—needs to fashion his or her current approach according to a rationale that makes sense to him/herself. Only then can a therapist follow the steps in the back-and-forth between him/ herself and the patient, correct mis-steps with an appropriate degree of flexibility, and do as little therapeutic harm and confer as much benefit as possible. This will happen if, and only if, the therapist is being authentic. It takes time to develop *one's own* technique as someone conducting a therapeutic consultation, and it is better to do so from a position of naïve genuineness than self-imposed posturing.

The beginning therapist is mostly at sea. When helping such a person find his or her bearings, I encourage a certain *attitude* to the clinical work. To be sure, I try to help the trainee to reflect on the implications of doing or not doing this or that—for instance, shaking hands at the beginning and/or end of the consultation, using first names or surnames (for instance, to use first names alone might not only be presumptuous, but also prescribe a stance for each party), sitting in the chair furthest from or closest to the door, and so on. I also suggest certain parameters for the meeting and, in particular, advise that the therapist states clearly at the beginning that this is a consultation, that it will last for (say) 90 minutes, and that it is a self-contained process rather than a lead-in to more extended treatment. Beyond this, it seems to me, the therapist's attitude is the most important ingredient in what he or she brings to the consultation. At the heart of that attitude are compassion and a devotion to understand the person who comes for help.

In the beginning

An assessment consultation begins with a perceived need. One of the first questions is: whose need, and what kind(s) of need?

All being well, the patient's needs figure prominently. Having said this, it may be important to take account of the needs of the anxious GP, the concerned social worker, the perplexed psychiatrist, or, of course, the distressed or at-wits-end relative. Such experiences and needs at one remove may have diagnostic significance, but they are also important for establishing the context within which any intervention is planned.

There is also the question, often a related question, of "Why now?" What has prompted the referral, or evoked the patient's sense of need, at this particular time and juncture of his or her life?

Already, then, the process of assessing has begun. One might call this a pre-assessment, in the sense that an assessment *interview* with an identified patient has not yet taken place. Indeed, and as Jane Milton discussed in chapter 3, an interview may or may not be appropriate to address the presenting problem. So a therapist might respond to a referral letter by contacting the referrer, something that can result in the referral being withdrawn or directed elsewhere. This might be justified on the grounds that, for example, a person is too disturbed or insufficiently interested in a psychodynamic exploration of his or her problems. In this case, a psychoanalytic assessment interview might be harmful or wasteful. Alternatively, there might be malfunction in some interpersonal system within which the patient is embedded. For instance, there may be reason for believing that the place to start is with an assessment of the marital couple or family.

The referral letter can sometimes be very informative, and it may be accompanied by copies of previous medical or psychological reports. It has been really helpful to my NHS assessment consultations to have available questionnaires that are sent to patients on a routine basis. The questions concern such matters as the nature and history of a person's presenting problems and other medical and psychiatric history, the person's upbringing and family/partner relations from the past into the present, his or her employment history and job satisfaction, whether the person has sexual difficulties and negative feelings about his or her body, whether he or she takes medication, and any other matters he or she wishes to raise.

Broadly speaking, there are two ways in which referral letters and questionnaires provide valuable information. These represent two of the three classes of evidence that I discussed in chapter 1. First, they convey historical facts. Such facts include the patient's past and present medical and other problems, and, all being well, some facts about why the patient is seeking this kind of help at this particular point in time. They also include facts about the person's history of relationships and, in particular, whether there is evidence of relatively stable and satisfying relationships at least sometime during the person's life.

These facts are important for several reasons, and here I mention two. First, one needs to consider a person's "suitability" for psychotherapy in the context of that person's past and present circumstances, and other forms of support or treatment that might need to accompany psychotherapy. Many an individual who could manage, say, once-weekly psychotherapy in the context of having a supportive relationship or a steady job might find such treatment disorganizing and unhelpful under other circumstances. For others, psychotherapy needs to be considered in the context of medical cover, whether for medication or potential inpatient treatment in the event of crisis. The referral letter and questionnaire may prompt a psychotherapist to request further information about such matters.

Second, these kinds of fact contribute to a view of the patient's potential for disturbed states of mind on the one hand, and his or her ability to sustain relationships on the other. A person who has never managed to engage in and derive benefit from a consistent relationship, whether as a child or adult, is likely to encounter difficulty in being helped by a psychotherapist, especially when that psychotherapist is at the focus of highly conflicted feelings. Patients who have had multiple abortions, or cut themselves, or had alcohol or other drug problems, or report recurrent violent relationships, need to have these things understood and taken very seriously. Otherwise, they might easily become involved in a treatment that makes their problems worse. A valuable rule of thumb (also used by Jane Milton in the previous chapter) is that a patient will become as disturbed in psychotherapy as he or she has become most disturbed in the past.

Then there are other kinds of fact conveyed by the referral letter and questionnaire. These facts are less explicit, but they may be no less important. In the case of referral letters, sometimes one can glean how the referrer has experienced the patient, whether as someone eliciting sympathy, stirring anxiety or despair, or prompting other positive or negative feelings that the referrer is needing to deal with through the referral. Each such pattern of relatedness is likely to be capturing something about the patient's style of engaging in dependent relationships, as well as forewarning what may emerge in the patient's relations with a therapist.

Similarly, in reading questionnaires that patients have filled out, one has first-hand experience of the impact of the patient's communications. Some questionnaires tax the reader's patience with cramped, overflowing, joined-up script; others seem balanced and coherent, and evoke sympathy and concern; others are scant in detail, perhaps completed in capital letters and with blank sections just where one is most eager to learn of the patient's experience; and others are not returned at all.

Especially in relation to these kinds of fact, but to some degree in relation to all the facts that become available before and in the course of a consultation, it is important not to jump to conclusions. It is not easy *both* to take the facts seriously *and* to wait until one is in a better position to make informed judgements over what the facts mean. A therapist values these facts because they contribute to knowledge of the patient, yet alone they do not amount to such knowledge. They provide an important part of the context within which all other facts will come to be understood. Yet the interpretation of the hardest of facts is influenced by what happens in the therapeutic encounter.

A framework in mind

I began as a trainee, and somewhere along the line I became a trainee-no-longer. I hope this did not mean I stopped learning from presenting my work to others—in fact, I know I didn't stop learning—but I had arrived at my way of and conducting assessment consultation. Or perhaps I should say, my ways of conducting consultations, because it is clear to me that I do different things in relation to different patients with different needs. Anyway, as I crossed the blurred boundary from trainee to trainer, I acquired a fresh responsibility. I felt that I should not only have, but also be able to articulate, good reasons for doing or saying—or indeed, not doing or not saying—*anything* as a therapist. True, this was and remains an aspiration rather than an accomplishment, but I take it to apply to any and all moments of an assessment consultation.

Of course, one might sometimes be misled into supposing that one's reasons for saying this or that are good, when they are not. Beyond this, one is bound to be caught up in enacting roles that at least temporarily overwhelm one's capacity to reason. As I shall illustrate, this is an inevitable part of being a psychotherapist. Yet as a professional, one should apply one's skills in a disciplined way. This means knowing what one is doing, knowing the point in what one is doing, and believing that doing this for this reason is in the best interests of the patient.

There are two qualifications to be made here. The first concerns what it means to "say something" and "do something". It is a moot point, one discussed by psychoanalysts concerned with the therapeutic action of analysis, how far the specific content of a therapist's interpretations is important for conferring insight, and how far their significance lies in the attitude the interpretations convey. Here, I focus on the therapist's attitude as embodying the personal aspect of interpersonal understanding.

In any consultation, it matters that, for enough of the time, a therapist is emotionally available to the patient and what the patient expresses and enacts. This does not mean that the therapist is totally exposed, nor is at a patient's mercy. Rather, the therapist needs to be able to register and encompass what a patient is expressing and communicating and to digest the emotional experience in the service of therapeutic progress. Whether or not the therapist says something about this, or does something like grunting or nodding or pausing, is often less important than what such statements and non-verbal communications convey about the therapist's capacity to take things on board. From a complementary perspective, what a therapist says or does can be as clever as you like, but unless such sayings and doings are grounded in something like emotional understanding, then they are likely to be of little consequence (or worse).

The second qualification concerns the best interests of the patient. Here I want to expand on a theme I introduced in chapter 1. In some quarters, it is taken to be a relatively straightforward matter to identify what the patient wants and needs. For instance, pretty well any patient who attends an NHS organization to find help with his or her emotional difficulties is going to want a sympathetic hearing and, if possible, reassurance and support. The patient also has a right to have the consultation explained in advance and to object if he or she feels that what is offered differs from what is sought.

A moment's reflection suggests that the situation is not so simple. Consider the case of a patient who presents not to a psychotherapist, but to a physician or surgeon. This patient, too, would prefer to have sympathy, reassurance, and support. But far more important, he or she wants to be diagnosed and treated appropriately. I recall an occasion when, with fellow medical students, I was in the emergency room of a London hospital, standing at the bedside of someone who had suffered a car accident. We gingerly touched the patient's badly bruised face. Then the on-duty doctor came in, took hold of the patient's upper jaw, and gently but firmly pulled it forward to reveal the serious fracture that had disconnected this bony structure from the rest of the skull. Lesson learnt. Even when circumstances are less dramatic, a patient who does not want to experience pain is prepared to do so if it is necessary with a view to achieving longer-term gain.

I stress, *if it is necessary*. Putting anyone in a position of unnecessary and fruitless suffering is inexcusable. However, sometimes, it *is* necessary to discover the degree of disturbance a patient can experience. Only in this way can one provide the professional service that the patient seeks and requires.

The acid test is whether what one does is in the patient's best interests. Several considerations are relevant. First, there are two parties who need to make decisions. The patient needs to know what psychotherapeutic treatment might mean. I have already said that in an effective psychotherapy, a person is likely to become as disturbed as he or she has the potential to become. The patient needs to know this, in order to decide whether to embark on this troubling, perhaps intermittently disabling, treatment. The therapist needs to know this, too, and to weigh up whether treatment is likely to contain the disturbance and promote the person's development. So if one needs both therapist and patient to arrive at an informed view of the risks and benefits of treatment, how can an initial consultation contribute to meeting this need?

It seems to me that a prime focus of a psychotherapy consultation is assessing the balance between a person's level of potential disturbance and his or her ability to harness the power of the therapeutic relationship to get through turbulent times. I have known very troubled patients who have remarkable resolve and determination to pursue what is true and emotionally honest, and who have used the therapist's understanding to endure the pain and disturbance that facing need and conflict has entailed. I have known far less troubled patients who have little interest or investment in facing their emotional realities, and who avoid and evade almost anything that provokes conflict or distress.

At the end of the day, and whether or not a person is offered psychotherapy, it is for the patient to decide his or her own stance over these matters. All a therapist can or should do in a consultation is to point out where in the conduct of the patient's emotional life (including the life of the session) the patient is making choices of which he or she is only partly aware, or only partly able to identify, and to lay out what follows for the person's relationships and emotional life. Often, from the perspective of what a therapist can show a patient, this is the limit of one's remit.

Here I could move on to discuss how shifts in relational stance between patient and therapist provide essential grist to the mill of the consultation process. For example, they provide opportunities for the therapist to point out how, at a given moment, the patient is *choosing* to move in this direction rather than that in dealing with feelings that have just been aroused. Instead, I shall postpone discussion of such matters and illustrate how I begin assessment consultations. And here I repeat: I do not suggest that novice trainees, nor anyone who feels more than task-appropriate kinds of discomfort, should try to do what I shall describe. My hope is that the account will illustrate some principles that may be relevant for psychotherapy assessment consultations, however these are conducted.

The first few minutes

The title of this section echoes that of chapter 11 in my father's book *Forms of Feeling* (R. F. Hobson, 1985)—namely, "The First Five Minutes". Like my father before me, I believe that within the first 5 or 10 minutes of meeting a person who comes for a psychotherapy consultation, there open out vistas on that person's emotional world that are arresting, intriguing, often moving, and sometimes shocking.

Yet one does not know where the beginning may lead. As T. S. Eliot wrote in *Four Quartets*: ". . . what you thought you came for / Is only a shell, a husk of meaning / From which the purpose breaks only when it is fulfilled / If at all." The first 5 or 10 minutes of a consultation may contain much that is pivotal for understanding a patient's predicament, but those initial minutes do not yield that understanding. We can mentally record what happens, but we do not know what is significant, nor how it is significant. All we can presume, albeit with an appropriate degree of qualification, is that what is happening holds the key to much that we and the patient need to know and that we and the patient need to work on. The therapist's hope is that by the end of the consultation, the meaning of what transpires at the beginning will become clear.

In preparation for the assessment interview, I arrange two chairs at approximately 45 degrees to each other, with a table just to one side. My chair is the one farthest from the door, so that the patient can feel that he or she is not trapped—and so that (*very* rarely) a troubled patient can walk out unhindered. I always put on a tie as symbolic acknowledgement that, however intimate, this is a meeting within a formal framework. My role is that of a professional clinician, not a friend.

When I greet the patient at the lift, I do so by stating the patient's title and surname ("Mr Brown?"), and introduce myself as Dr Hobson (neither "Peter Hobson", nor "Professor Hobson"). I lead the way to the interview room, adjusting my pace as I pass down the corridor so that the patient can easily follow behind, although (significantly) some patients choose to walk abreast. I open the door for the patient and indicate the chair. Once we are both seated, I repeat that my name is Dr Hobson and say that this is a preliminary assessment consultation and that we have until such-and-such a time, usually 90 minutes from the start. If the patient has been late, I say that I had set aside 90 minutes, so now we have only so much time left before the end. If this has happened, then at some point I return to what it means for the patient to have lost—whether by intention, neglect, or unforeseen circumstance—potentially precious time.

Then I wait, looking at the patient intently and steadily, but not aggressively. Invariably, tension rises sharply.

I do not impose silence, although for a few moments (sometimes longer) I am silent myself. Nor do I allow the patient's anxiety or aggression to mount to unmanageable levels. If needs be, I move swiftly to comment on what I judge the patient to be experiencing in my stance, trying to state only as much as I can on the basis of the evidence available.

When the situation is especially tense, there is usually enough in the very first comments the patient makes to provide a clue as to whether he or she is feeling that *I* am aggressive, unhelpful, unreasonable, sadistic, manipulative, or whatever. When the situation is less tense, there is breathing and thinking space to see how the patient's experiences unfold, and how the patient makes adjustments, before I make a comment. Often the patient is unsettled but is able to gather him/herself and talk to me (and I am listening intently) with more or less candour. In other cases, the patient launches into an account as if, to all intents and purposes, I am being facilitating, helpful, and understanding—or perhaps, on one level only, as if I hardly matter at all.

I select two features from this condensed overview for further comment. First, there are marked individual differences in how different patients are stirred up by this challenging and potentially threatening and/or uncomfortable situation. No doubt at all, it *is* challenging, for both patient and therapist. The patient comes vulnerable and needy and is not being provided with kindly reassurance nor the safety net of questions to answer.

Second, and what justifies my style of assessment consultation, the approach often yields explicit if transitory indication both of the quality and degree of a person's potential disturbance *and* of the patient's manner of dealing with that disturbance. The ensuing period will uncover further detail about the patient's experience of myself in those early moments. More than this, it will reveal how far the patient is able to allow and/or recruit my serious attempts to understand his or her experience, and how far this alters and deepens the nature of our personal engagement.

I would re-state that, by and large, although not always, this way of conducting the early part of a consultation makes manifest the quality and degree of a patient's potential disturbance. There are, of course, many qualities of disturbance, and one especially important distinction (originating in the work of Klein and Fairbairn) is between paranoid-schizoid and depressive-position functioning (for further detail, see chapter 10). As described in my postscript to chapter 1, the paranoid-schizoid state of mind corresponds with the world of nightmare or fairy-tale, where a person experiences malevolent and intrusive figures alongside others that may be unrealistically idealized. The atmosphere is charged with threats to one's very being from invasive and persecuting quasi-human forces. The depressive position is different in quality, because here the primary anxiety is that of experiencing loss of, or harm done to, needed and caring as well as cared-for figures, experienced as whole people with a subjectivity of their own. Here, too, accompanying anxieties and conflicts may be very painful, but they are different in kind. The opening moments of the consultation can tap more or less straight into whichever of these contrasting states of mind predominate in a patient.

This is not an either–or situation. Given suitable circumstances, almost all of us have the potential to find ourselves in paranoid-schizoid as well as depressive-position frames of mind. The degree and preponderance of paranoid-schizoid functioning is very important for the psychotherapy assessment, as is the entrenchment of certain other ways of conducting an emotional and interpersonal life, such as the perverse or narcissistic.

One index of the quality and degree of a person's fall-back state of mind is *what* becomes overt in those first moments of the interview. The sense of mutual persecution and threat may be tangible. Another index is *how long* the disturbance lasts. In rare instances, debilitating disturbance accompanied by caginess, aggressiveness, persecution, and threat can maintain a grip on proceedings for half an hour or longer. In such a state, the patient is likely to experience the therapist's words as so many incoming bullets. In other patients, tension and hostility rapidly diminish as the patient comes to experience me as trying to understand rather than attack or manipulate him or her for my own ends. In others again, only hints of disturbance can be discerned, and these patients seem to deal with these right from the start. One may gain the impression that the person can call on internal resources to support thinking and sustain the hope of receiving thoughtfulness and help. On the other hand, there might be disquieting gaps in the patient's repertoire of feeling. Here one needs to be careful, because it is important not to miss ominous signs that seeming equanimity reflects a kind of emptiness that betokens underlying splits in a person's emotional life.

Thus far, my description has set disturbance centre-stage. This could be misleading, insofar as the most disturbed picture is relatively *un*common among the patients I see in my NHS practice. If this were not the case, I might well modify my approach (see also chapter 9). The point of what I do is not merely nor principally to allow *very* disturbed states of mind to become manifest and available for joint work in the consultation. Rather, my aim is to illuminate and provide a basis for working on a whole range of less disturbed states of mind and, more specifically, to explore *with* a patient the nature of his or her *clear and present* anxieties, conflicts, and defences.

Before I turn to case examples to illustrate the point, I will conclude this part of the chapter with a true and telling story. This concerns a person I assessed many years ago. The consultation is seared on my memory.

> The patient was a middle-aged man referred with a seemingly minor bodily disorder. He had received nine months of dynamic psychotherapy some years previously. So, as far as one could tell from these and other indicators, he was *not* terribly troubled and was a candidate for further treatment. I met this man and embarked on the interview as already described. Within about five seconds of my falling silent, his eyes bulged and he froze into an acutely psychotic state. I immediately intervened and spent the rest of the consultation talking him down towards a state more like that in which he had arrived.

> It turned out that this patient knew he was very troubled. He also knew that his previous psychotherapy had skimmed over this fact. Not only this, but he described how his disturbance was somehow connected with the early months of his life, when he was brought up in an orphanage.

> It is possible to consider and evaluate this consultation from various perspectives. One remains most vivid in my memory: in the course of our meeting, this patient and I together confronted an alarming truth.

The following brief clinical vignettes (as well as some of those that follow in subsequent chapters) are intended to illustrate what happens at the beginning of assessment consultations. They are not representative, but neither are they exceptional. They are just what happened when these particular patients arrived and sat down. In different ways, the beginnings of their consultations were very revealing. The cases are intended to illustrate how consultations move through different levels of meaning and can reveal differences in what might seem to be similar modes of clinical presentation. Each of the next three patients below keeps his or her thinking on an abstract plane, and his or her contact with myself correspondingly unspecific. Yet beneath this similarity, they show marked individual differences.

Case vignette: Mr A

Mr A was a man in his early forties who was referred for "symptoms of anxiety and low mood", an inability to feel or express enthusiasm, and a pervading sense of dissatisfaction with himself and his achievements. He was said to drift from one thing to another.

Mr A arrived on time. He was carrying a coffee. Once in the consulting room, he put the coffee down with the comment that he would be ready to drink by the end of our meeting, and then he sat, initially in a passive way, staring at me. I said that he appears to be waiting. He said that he does not know what to expect, he has not done this before. After a further pause, I said that he seems to expect me to take the lead. He said that he presumed it was my "tactic", so as not to interfere with what was to happen. He finds my approach "challenging", but at the same time he indicated that he was managing to work out what was happening. He said that it reminded him of when he was in the sixth form: he used to look through a cardboard tube at other people, and observe them, and it is strange what one sees.

When I commented on the unpleasant edge to his experience, he more or less dismissed what I said and gave an abstract and rather elaborate set of reflections about his understanding of what was happening. He said he came here interested in what a professional might have to say about him.

I took up how not only did he experience me as observing him in this detached manner, offering him little help despite the unusualness of the situation, but so, too, he was observing me observing him in this way. For example, he was anticipating what I might have to offer him, in such a way that he could reflect on this and find it "interesting".

This initial, cagey part of our meeting lasted for quite some time, perhaps between 10 and 15 minutes. Then I pointed out how he comes for serious reasons, but engaging with him on a personal level—or indeed, he introducing personal things about himself—seem not to have been happening so far. It emerged that not only was he half-removed from what was happening, but he was also finding it "quite amusing". The onus was on me to tap into the seriousness of the situation that brought him here.

I want to interrupt the account at this point to make two observations. All this might sound intellectual and cool. Even at the time, it felt laboured as I held to my task of discerning and articulating what I thought our current engagement entailed, at a level that was accessible to Mr A and myself. I believe that there was explicit evidence for every observation or statement I made—evidence I could cite to Mr A, as and when I needed to do so. There was no rocket science here. Although much that I have described illustrates Mr A's defensiveness, I also acted upon something generated in the countertransference—namely, the need for *me* to lay myself on the line, and to take a risk, in commenting on his serious reasons for coming and *my* serious attitude towards these reasons, when Mr A could not do so himself. To return to my report:

> As the session progressed, there emerged fleeting and then increasingly longer periods of time when Mr A was more directly engaged with me. But each time, he would move away to more abstract reflections, humorous asides, or other more distanced positions (which, incidentally, I tended to track explicitly). He acknowledged that I was right in saying that his way of coping with emotional stress was something that, while it served him well on one level, also created a "bubble" around him that distanced himself from more alive engagement. I took up how his talking about things appears to happen in a way that contributes to, rather than punctures, the bubble that he creates. It is a real difficulty, here and now, that the means to understanding—his very ways of talking and thinking—can be used in that way.

I will break off the account at this point. By the end of the session, Mr A had become less controlling and more alive in his engagement, and he had responded to my request for a dream (which happened to be both revealing and obscure). It also became possible to sense some of the anxiety against which Mr A was protecting himself, especially his fear of change if he did not have certainty about what change would mean. In a follow-up interview, he was movingly candid about his fragile self-esteem, as well as other matters. He clearly appreciated the work we had done, and he sought psychoanalytic psychotherapy.

Note how it took detailed and persistent work *of a particular kind* to analyse Mr A's manoeuvring of me, and his "observing" stance, in order to access something more personal and vulnerable about him. This involved my giving unrelenting attention to the transference and countertransference—as well as sustaining a commitment to being engaged with Mr A as he was experiencing myself and the situation from one moment to the next. Nothing was allowed to distract from, nor interfere with, this task.

Case vignette: Ms B

Here is a patient who has very different reasons for devoting effort to keep herself on an abstract level. Ms B is trying to construct and maintain some kind of coherent self.

Ms B was referred for depression and relationship difficulties. She did not attend when originally referred. When re-referred, she failed to send in the questionnaire. Then she telephoned at the time the interview was scheduled to begin, leaving the message that she was on her way, but lost. In the event, she arrived 15 minutes late.

When I collected her from the lift, Ms B stumbled over whether to call me Mr or Dr Hobson, and she half looked away. Once in the room, she looked at me rather blankly and said that if she were to say what she had been thinking about on the way, it would be that she is "numb". Something is wrong with her functioning, it's as if (and here she gestured) she is living on one level but there is something wrong (implying, I think, that this was unconnected with other levels of herself). She said she is a "survivor" in that, like others, she does somehow get through, but that seems to be all she is doing.

I took up how something similar seemed to be happening in this meeting. I said that she felt very uncertain what it was that I wanted from her—and this clearly unsettled her—so she tries to provide something articulate without being too personal. She agreed with this. Then what happened over the coming 20 minutes or so was that, again and again, Ms B would speak in a seemingly articulate way, but one that was abstract and lacking in personal depth. When, on prompting, she made an attempt to begin to talk about herself, she said something about moving from continent to continent but then fell silent and looked down. It seemed as if her mind was simply unable to function.

Rather than describing how this consultation unfolded, I shall pick up the story at the beginning of the subsequent follow-up interview.

Ms B began by complaining that the light was too bright (although one blind was partially closed, so that the light was shaded). When I hesitated a moment, she asked to change seats with me. I declined this request but did lower the blind. She said she wished she had her sunglasses with her—and as I took up with her, this seemed a concrete expression of her both wishing to shield herself from my sight (with me as potentially invasive, as she acknowledged, but also seeing her when she was not in control), and also to keep her in a darkened space, as if shielded from herself. On the other hand, particularly later on, she had a coherence of feeling and an ability to think about herself that surprised and impressed me.

Here we see a more troubled person, struggling to establish and maintain some kind of equilibrium. When other patients present with similar kinds of "concrete" behaviour—the manifest signs of disorientation, the uncertainty over what to call me, the reactions to the light, the wish to change seats—they can cause considerable disorientation in a therapist. In fact, Ms B evoked sympathy and dismay in me, rather than confusion and imbalance. As ever, here-and-now interpersonal engagement yielded emotional evidence about the patient's functioning, as only here-and-now engagements can.

My third case example provides a further contrast.

Case vignette: Mr C

Mr C was a middle-aged man who had been referred for low self-esteem and feeling depressed.

He arrived 5 minutes late. He gave me a diffident look with his handshake and then immediately apologized about his running late. He was plainly dressed for work.

He quickly registered that I was not going to be asking him questions, and he proceeded to say how he had come because there are things he wishes to change. Although he's had psychotherapy that has given him insights, it has not changed this "responses" to situations. He went on to say that he carries fear around with him, especially of people in authority. He said that perhaps he should change his aims in life, or settle for the way things are, but he wants things to be different.

Having referred to his difficulty as "it", he then extended the "it" to a much broader domain, and he referred to some times when he almost wonders whether it (meaning life) is worth it. He said that he's not very sociable.

Even at this early stage, I was struck by how Mr C related seemingly important things about himself without taking up a stance over whether they were important or not. It was impossible to tell whether they left him feeling this way or that, or, indeed, quite what significance they held.

Mr C proceeded to tell me about some of the ways he understood the impact of his mother's critical attitude and his father's relative unavailability, leaving him wishing to avoid conflict and friction. Beyond this, however, he tended to see his difficulties as matters of conditioning. And as he expressed it later, if he could apply rational thinking to his situation, this might bring change.

The prime focus of our meeting, then, even from the early part of the consultation, concerned Mr C's inability and/or unwillingness to connect himself to any particular view or feeling or judgement or thought. He would not allow himself to be seen to take up a stance that might be subject to criticism or external appraisal.

This was not just a matter of cognitive style. Both the nature and the effects of Mr C's emotional stance were reflected in an overly civilized interaction with myself. He did not object to my expecting him to talk; he always came up with reflective (typically abstract) thoughts about himself; he seemed to listen to what I was saying; and rarely did he disagree. On the face of it, he was both compliant and available.

Yet I had a strong sense that nothing much was happening, nor would things change. Here, in the transference, and on an interpersonal plane, we were immobilized in a world of spectral forms.

I rendered some of this explicit and did my best to anchor what I said to specific issues that arose in our exchanges. For example, I said how Mr C's initial description of himself was very matter-of-fact. Yet, I continued, there was also a sense of his potential deep unhappiness and even despair—for example, when he talked of how he has his dreams for the future, and if these were taken away, what would he be left with? For a moment, Mr C seemed to register what I was saying, and he acknowledged its truth. Yet all that followed was that Mr C turned back to abstract ways of thinking, and the potential value of addressing the specifics of his feelings was never realized.

I will add one detail from a later part of the consultation. Towards the end of our meeting, I asked Mr C if he could tell me a dream. He described a dream in which *he was with his current girlfriend, but also meeting with his first. He spent time with each, and was supposed to choose between the two, but nothing else happened.*

Even on the surface, this dream, and the inconsequentiality of what transpired in the dream, corresponds so closely to what had become apparent even in the early moments of the consultation. The dream and its telling led nowhere in particular, so, in a way, the dream contained a picture of itself (showing how the dream and its telling would remain but a shell, a husk of meaning). Yet it was also the case that, within the dream, there is indication of Mr C having a role in generating the seemingly helpless and hopeless state in which he found himself. In Mr C's

case, however, despite making every effort to encourage movement over the course of the session, there was little to indicate
that psychotherapy could alter his pervasive immobility.

Final reflections

In each of the vignettes I have given, the patient was avoiding and/
or controlling what might have been intimate engagement with
myself. Intimacy brings peril: one can be mistreated, neglected,
abandoned, invaded, punished, or found wanting. Intimate
engagement brings other challenges. In order to receive help from
someone else, for example, one has to acknowledge dependency
and a painful truth: one is not the source of all goodness. So it is
very common, and in a certain respect necessary, that in assessment
consultations patients protect themselves. No wonder, too, if they
become angry. This can be a sign of healthy engagement and
self-assertion. The question is this: what is the cost of a patient's
particular ways of managing his or her particular anxieties, and
what is his or her underlying capacity to establish the kind of
relationship that he or she needs in order to develop?

Early in chapter 1, I stressed that there is no single way to conduct
an assessment consultation. Therefore, one might ask: "Why make
the interview so stressful?" Surely the dangers and challenges I
have just mentioned are even more alarming for someone who is
vulnerable, and who comes in need of help.

I ask myself this question on a regular basis. And I have tried
other ways. I have begun consultations with a more overtly friendly
and sympathetic stance, and I have even tried to answer a patient's
questions about what the assessment interview will involve, and
what he or she is supposed to do. The problem is that I find that
such an approach leaves me substantially less able to judge the
qualities of a patient's emotional difficulties on the one hand, and
his or her strengths on the other. I am left guessing about both the
patient's ability to use the therapist's help when the therapist is also
a source of disturbance, and the patient's willingness to join with
the therapist in addressing uncomfortable or distasteful facts. These
are important things to know when forecasting the likely outcome
of psychotherapy.

I realize that other psychotherapists will take a very different view. I have known an eminent psychotherapist who felt able to make dynamic formulations based on standard psychiatric reports, with no evidence from moment-by-moment transactions in therapeutic sessions. For myself, I would have almost nothing useful to say under such circumstances. There is a difference between speculation and judgement, and my aim is to speculate as little as possible. This means that I focus on what I experience first-hand, under the disciplined conditions afforded by the setting of a consultation. This in turn means that I need to have direct access to expressions of "the unconscious". When I take what might *seem* a more facilitating stance early in the interview, too much remains hidden. If I ask questions, all I get is answers. Those answers are framed in relation to what the patient is concluding I am after. The answers may be intended to supply what I want, or to thwart what I want, or to achieve any manner of aims, but it is nigh impossible to track what is really going on.

I believe my stance *is* facilitating, but in a different way. Freud's comparison between the psychoanalyst and the surgeon has relevance here. A surgeon has to do what he or she has to do. Patients come for a professional service when they attend an assessment consultation, and they are aware that the process of getting what they need may be taxing. Almost certainly, for therapist as well as patient, taxing it will be.

The beginning is only the beginning. What happens next? The initial events of the consultation need to be set in context. This brings us, in chapter 5, to the middle phase of a consultation.

Working over

R. Peter Hobson

A s a consultation proceeds, things that have happened at the beginning of the session need to be worked over, as patterns of anxiety and conflict, defence, and relatedness repeat and resurface in different forms, again and again. Each time they do, a therapist's picture of the patient acquires depth. Whatever disturbance and distress erupted at the commencement of the interview is now set in the context of other, often more reflective states of mind that the patient may bring to bear on making sense of what his or her feelings mean. The picture is also enriched by what the person recounts about his or her past and present life.

In psychotherapy, as in life, all is in movement. A particular form of movement is especially important as an expression of a patient's ways of dealing with anxieties and conflicts stirred by an intimate relationship. This kind of movement involves shifts in intersubjective engagement. Such shifts entail that patient and therapist *feel* how things alter in relation to one other. Although the determinants of the respective positions of therapist and patient are complex, the attitudes of each have a shaping influence on the attitudes of the other. Psychotherapists need to hone their awareness of how they are being induced to feel things, as well as how their own attitudes and interventions influence a patient's state of mind.

This view of psychotherapeutic transactions has obvious implications for a therapist's technique. Not only does the therapist learn things from his or her emotional response to what the patient brings (the countertransference)—a special kind of learning that yields a special kind of knowledge—but, also, the therapist has an opportunity to track movements in the relative emotional positions of him/herself and the patient. These shifts can reveal what stirs the patient's anxiety or hostility or vulnerability, insofar as movement may be prompted by what has been happening—and what is perceptible—in the current encounter. "What has been happening" might refer to what the therapist has just said or not said, or to what the patient has just thought or felt, or what has been evoked on some less easily articulated but noticeable level. Along with this, shifts make manifest a patient's attempts both to configure his or her own mind and to moderate or manage feelings stirred in the course of the patient–therapist exchanges.

This focus on movements in relational stance entails that the therapist is ever alert to his or her *feel* of what is happening from moment to moment in the patient–therapist relation. It tends to mean that what the therapist notices and chooses to remark upon are seemingly simple states and processes for which there is immediate evidence. To some people, it may seem almost trivial for a therapist to point out that when he picked up what the patient had just said, the patient turned her eyes away; it might appear superficial for the therapist to comment on the patient's circumlocutions and abstractions when asked about her early life; or it could be thought laboured for the therapist to suggest that the patient was trying to conceal her irritation at the therapist's behaviour. Yet frequently such moments contain a wealth of emotional meaning. In addition, they reveal avenues to explore and negotiate what *the patient* is prepared and able to reflect upon and find meaningful.

Such interventions by the therapist amount to new and challenging relational events. The patient has done something that is emotionally significant, and the therapist has registered and commented on this. Now the patient has to deal with the therapist's contribution and with how it has affected their respective stances. Patients may feel that the therapist has helped them to get hold of something that slipped past their notice, or is reprimanding them for avoiding things; they may feel that the therapist is providing helpful support and nourishment, or seducing and subjugating them; they may experience the therapist as sensitive, or as missing the point entirely; and so on, through infinite varieties of experience and emotional state. And in relation to each feeling about the therapist and the therapist's attitude and behaviour, of course, the patient has complexly interwoven states of mind, whether envious or grateful, combative or submissive, confident or vulnerable, and so on.

In each such moment, too, there are overarching issues of whether, from the patient's perspective, the person of the therapist is for me or against me, emotionally available or shut off, exploitative or beneficent, trustworthy or untrustworthy, able to stand emotional storms or fragile and without boundaries, sane or mad. Such are a few, very basic dimensions of relational life. Whenever possible, they need to be identified and understood.

In therapeutic focus

Perhaps it is churlish to ask: "Why?" Why do these things need to be identified and understood? Why not just let them be, and instead of addressing such stuff as dreams are made on, adopt a more down-to-earth strategy? Would it not be better to provide a clear therapeutic structure, make systematic enquiries, and apply techniques that assist the patient to control and alter his or her behaviour?

It depends what one means by "better". Yes, other approaches might lead to therapeutic benefit. That is an empirical matter, and one that requires sophisticated research. What I want to stress is that the kinds of relational pattern I have cited do not go away. If a patient's difficulties are intimately bound up with such relations, then it makes sense to turn the spotlight on the relational aspect of the problem. If personal relations are central and play a causative role in leading to someone's distress or disturbance, as often they do, then almost certainly they will need to be addressed if significant change is to occur.

It is worth noting something about the therapeutic stance and focus that I have been advocating. The approach conforms with the classical psychoanalytic idea that, broadly speaking, it may be advantageous to work from surface to depth in addressing relational issues, or to analyse resistance before exploring underlying content. The idea is that one should start with what is immediately available and close to a patient's consciousness and only subsequently point out deeper, unconscious meanings. I do not see things quite this way, because much of what is on the surface is *also* deep. Often a psychotherapist needs to draw attention to profound personal issues that are expressed in and through a patient's manifest expressive and communicative patterns. Yet at certain points and with certain patients, movement may become possible only when underlying anxieties or conflicts are addressed.

Then comes the next question: how might we alter the patient's propensity to engage in less than satisfying, and sometimes outright destructive, patterns of relatedness, whether towards other people or towards him/herself? As the title of this chapter indicates, I think of the process as "working over". Working over is more than a matter of going over. Even in a consultation, the process is developmentally orientated and concerns the promotion of change, however small or momentary. This means that we need to consider the processes of therapeutic change and how a therapist might foster these processes.

Psychoanalytic psychotherapists work from *within* relational goings-on. The principle is grounded in developmental theory discussed earlier (chapter 1) and, in particular, the notion that certain critical capacities of mind develop through interpersonal and, more specifically, intersubjective experience. If one is to manage difficult feelings, then one needs to have available, either within one's own mind or in an interpersonal setting, the resources to do so. The idea is that people for whom psychotherapy might be beneficial are those who need help of a certain kind *from another person* in order to develop through and out of a current problematic state.

It is easy enough to contrast such a position with other theories and therapeutic approaches that either create or endorse a split between the patient and his or her difficulties. For instance, someone practising interpersonal therapy (Weissman, Markowitz,

& Klerman, 2007) tends to set up an alliance between him/herself and a depressed patient, so together they can discuss symptoms as a kind of recalcitrant, quasi-external bit of pathology. More challenging is the task of delineating the *variety* of ways in which interpersonal influences may effect change within the domain of psychoanalytic work.

Broadly speaking, one might draw a contrast between two states of affairs. The first applies to patients who have a relatively coherent sense of themselves. For these individuals, the process of psychotherapy is a bit like discovering what was always known. Not infrequently, a patient will say this towards the end of psychotherapy, or even at the end of a consultation. What the patient also indicates is that what he or she kind of knew before is now known in a new way. The new way has allowed the patient to free up feelings and mental capacities that had been segregated off and, for this reason, were unavailable. When patients in this group use other people to carry parts of themselves (through projective identification) and operate in this way during a consultation, the business of helping them recognize and take responsibility for what had been disowned may be relatively straightforward.

In such cases, psychoanalytic psychotherapy can be seen as providing conditions in which hindrances to natural development are diminished. Racker (1968) follows Freud in citing the French surgeon's motto: "*Je le pansai, Dieu le guérit*" [I have dressed his wounds, God cured him]. It is a wonder to behold how, once blocks to movement and growth have been shifted, a person may gather developmental momentum. Often a psychotherapist has to do just enough, and no more, for God to take care of the rest.

The second state of affairs applies to patients who are more seriously troubled and fragmented. Here the process of helping a patient to reintegrate highly dispersed parts of him/herself may be time-consuming, gruelling, and only partially successful. In these cases, the dispersion is effected by the patient's more entrenched and sometimes diffused forms of projective identification. In addition, such patients tend to have difficulty thinking with symbols (a matter discussed by Joanne Stubley in chapter 8). One of the tasks to be faced, therefore, is to create conditions in which, however gradually, the patient acquires the means both to tolerate what has been intolerable and to think about what has been unthinkable.

It is beyond the remit of this book to discuss the therapeutic action of psychoanalytic psychotherapy. Suffice it to emphasize a principle that underpins much of the clinical work described in this book, and one that applies in different ways to almost all patients. This is that if a therapist can register and contain feelings induced by, and often belonging to, a patient, where those feelings are unmanageable to the patient in isolation, then this provides an interpersonal basis for integration and change. Development will require more than this—it is not true that "all you need is love"—but containment and the accompanying understanding and commitment to truth may prove to be a *sine qua non* for many a psychoanalytic psychotherapy.

Let me return to the natural history of consultation interviews. In a consultation, the story unfolds in a sequence of steps. The steps are constituted by shifts in the mutually responsive stances of patient and therapist. They may be few in number—for instance, when patient and therapist become locked in a sadomasochistic clinch from which it is difficult to escape. Or they may be many, as a patient responds to the stance embodied in each of the therapist's interpretations, and the therapist in turn adjusts and then adjusts again to the patient's utterances and non-verbal communications.

I shall illustrate just a few among many factors that a therapist might have an opportunity to assess as a consultation proceeds. Perhaps that is not the best way to express matters, because, all being well, the consultation throws up *which* factors are those that demand immediate attention. These differ from one individual to another. In the cases that follow, special attention is given to discovering activity in passivity and to assessing a patient's commitment to discovering the truth. I shall make some preliminary remarks about these two aspects of the interviews.

Activity and passivity

One of the most intriguing facets of the psychoanalytic enterprise is to study the interface between what a person passively experiences and what he or she actively generates. Freud considered that a central aim of psychoanalysis is to extend the domain over which a person can exercise agency. This is part of the grand design, to make what is unconscious conscious. If successful, a patient's neurotic misery may be turned into common unhappiness, so that he or she might find fulfilment in love, work, and play.

An assessment consultation can be like walking a tightrope. On one side is what the patient knows, and knows that he or she knows. This is the realm of deliberation and decision-making. The patient chooses which bed to lie in, and so be it. On the other side is what the patient experiences as "happenings". These might include emotional storms, impulsive thoughts or actions, anxieties and depression, misfortunes in relationships, feelings of unfulfilment, psychosomatic disorders, and so on.

It would afford the patient little advantage if the consultation deviated far to one or other side of the tightrope. If much of the time were spent in the realm of what is conscious, the patient would do better seeing what folks in California call a "life coach"; if much of the time were spent interpreting what used to be called the "deep unconscious", you might as well be whistling in the wind. The patient will not know what you are talking about. What is deeply unconscious is deeply unconscious.

But here, on the tightrope, one can look down to either side and see that all is not so clearly divided. An assessing psychotherapist is in a position to help a patient see that the line between what is and is not the patient's responsibility is less than definitive. Moreover, it is drawn other than where it seems. In what the patient experiences passively, either as bolts from the blue or as buffetings from unseen forces, lies the patient's active connivance. The patient's choices are obscured, yet they are also obdurate. In what the patient sees as rational choice lie seams of self-delusion and distortion. These hidden or half-hidden facts are likely to emerge in the course of the consultation. Freud's notion of "resistance" is a blanket term that does scant justice to the ingenuity and variety of human means to evade perception of unwelcome realities.

It is remarkable that with the intervention of a psychotherapist, the cartography of the mind can change, sometimes radically. Even in a single consultation, one may help a patient discover some startling facts about his or her own role in creating and sustaining an unhappy emotional life.

I say "discover", but even the discovery is one that requires a patient to make choices. One can choose not to see. All one can do as a psychotherapist is to present the evidence of what needs to be seen, graphically and immediately before a patient's eyes. In that dramatic and suspenseful moment—or, more commonly, sequence of moments—the patient decides to move this way or that. The therapist follows the movement and either bides time before trying again (perhaps paying more attention to underlying anxieties) or joins the patient in moving forward.

There are several ways in which these critical junctures can be negotiated. Much depends on the patient's level of functioning and on what the patient needs the therapist to provide. At times, all it requires is firmness on the therapist's part. The therapist notices what happens, makes a comment on what has happened, and is not to be fobbed off. Some patients need a firm, steadying hand to address the truth. At other times, the process is more complicated. But let me give a simple example.

Many a time patients will come to psychotherapy stating that I (the therapist) am a doctor. They do not know about themselves. Their doctor sent them, they agreed, and now they want treatment, or at least advice. They adopt this position, for all the world expecting advice from the outset, even though they have not said anything about themselves, and it is they who have had years' first-hand experience of their own lives. Another version of this stance is for a patient to say that he or she does not know what is important, so I should ask questions.

My response is to point out that the patient is asking me (with the emphasis on "me"). This prompts either thoughtfulness or some defensive justification that yes, I am the expert. In the latter case, I say again, the patient calls me the expert, as if it is I who knows about the patient's own life. I might add that this is even before I have been told anything.

Why do I behave like this? It is so easy to allow someone to locate all the responsibility, doubt, uncertainty, complication, and struggle of *thinking* in someone else. In some patients, the process by which this is effected is so powerful that my observation makes little difference. In many others, there occurs an initially tentative but increasingly marked shift in the mental scenery. Someone who had seemed empty of thoughts suddenly begins to think. When this happens swiftly, it would be more accurate say that someone who at one moment disavows the capacity to think suddenly assumes responsibility for thought. This represents a mini-revolution, and one that portends well for what may follow.

Commitment to the truth

The discussion about activity and passivity blends into my next theme, which concerns commitment to the truth. Here I want to broaden the topic.

To hold as true is to hold as true of reality. Reality is a Godsend. It may not always seem so, but it is. How wonderful, we might imagine, to be like the White Queen in *Alice in Wonderland*, who could believe six impossible things before breakfast. But, on reflection, perhaps not so wonderful. Tempting though omnipotence might appear, it must be very scary. However much we detest the constraints and sometimes the sheer horribleness of reality, it is provides us with a stable home, a place to be. It remains exactly what it is, whatever we do.

But the stability and reassurance of that home comes at a price. We have to sign up to a deal. The deal is that reality demands our respect. We cannot, like the White Queen, choose to believe impossible things.

Yet we humans can bear only so much reality. Even when we know that evading or distorting reality costs us dearly, still we may find the prospect seductive and the ill-gotten gains too rewarding. Yet when we are helped both to see and to accept reality, we may choose to take the harder path. The implications may be profound.

Now some readers may be perplexed that this discussion appears in a chapter on working over rather than in the previous chapter, on the beginning of the consultation. Fair enough. The reason it appears here is that I want to show how the relational shifts I have described may represent the opening moves in a much longer, and deeply serious, game. At stake is how far the patient is willing as well as able to take the reins of his or her emotional life. I shall illustrate this through the following vignette.

Case vignette: Ms D

Ms D was a middle-aged woman who presented with relapsing depression and relationship difficulties.

Ms D arrived on time. She came out of the lift and gave me a firm handshake. On entering the room, she said how bright it was, how nice. On sitting down she became anxious and said, was I going to ask her questions? Or was I going to sit in silence? Did I mind if she further closed the blind (which was three-quarters closed) so it is less bright in her eyes? She proceeded to pull down the blind, then resumed her seat.

I remarked on how Ms D attempted to get our exchange going very quickly. She said that she does not mind silence with people she knows, but, yes, when she does not know "what someone is up to", she has to fill the gap. She also said how she finds it difficult to trust people.

Ms D went on to talk of her antidepressant medication and her ambivalence about this "numbing" her. She can go round and round in her mind, asking why she made the decisions she did in life. It seemed to me that perhaps this endless rumination was her own form of numbing self-medication, but for now I kept this thought to myself. Ms D also described herself as "confused".

Then, in a way that was to characterize a number of her statements in the first part of the interview, Ms D said that she has had to deal with life in the way she has. After all, she had to cope in difficult circumstances. Her subsequent description of her life as moving from one chaos to another threatened to become a description of the early part of the interview, as Ms D moved from one anxious thought to another, often conflicting anxious thought.

Our exchanges had an intense, unsettled, unresolvable back-and-forth quality. I took up with Ms D how she would react to my attempts to understand by half-acknowledging the truth of what I said but, at the same time, pushing me away. Sometimes this happened in gesture as well as in thought. Not only did she resist my attempts to connect with her, but also she did not want me to engage with troubling thoughts within her mind.

I said that Ms D conveyed how on the one hand she has a set of critical, or, as she put it, blaming attitudes towards herself. Then, on the other, she has another stance, in which she seems to be trying to justify her own ways of dealing with things. In addition, she seems to lack a belief in there being someone who would understand.

Yet there was something else happening. It was not difficult to sense that Ms D was available and interested when I took up what was going on. This was the case not only when addressing her vulnerability and helplessness, or the misery of her feeling herself to be stupid and useless, but also when I commented on the more active aggressive and blaming side to herself. True, Ms D led me to be careful in what I had to say. I found myself prepared for her to qualify my remarks. But at the same time I felt assured that there was a possibility of linking with her over what was true about her current situation.

This quality in the interview deepened as time went on. As Ms D herself was to acknowledge openly and convincingly, when she could hear that I was understanding her and speaking the truth to her—a truth that she said she already knew but had not put into words—then actually she did feel understood rather than attacked and manipulated. With this came relief. The relief was at least as intense when I was firm about Ms D's potentially destructive side, as when I expressed awareness of her vulnerability.

Such receptivity and commitment was most evident when I said things that at first Ms D did not understand. At one point, for example, I referred to there being a sadistic side to Ms D, as she gets caught up in an endless doubting and questioning of herself. She stopped me in order to clarify what I meant, then moved on thoughtfully.

What happened was not always straightforward, of course. There was one occasion where Ms D moved away from such engagement not to think further, but to bemoan the state in which she goes round and round in her head. This was an instance of what I call a self-representing event, because her description of going round and round applied to her activity in describing this very inclination. Her bemoaning was an instance of that which she was bemoaning, and this seemed to be a gratifying but destructive state of mind. Yet even here, it was possible to take this up and bring her back into a more meaningful exchange.

What it was possible to articulate, therefore, not only in Ms D's experience with others, but also in her own internal world, were various stances in which she was an active participant. She could be critical and relentlessly blaming; she had a different, more unsympathetic and uncomprehending side; and she could occupy a position in which she felt oppressed and unfairly judged. In addition to this, however, she had the capacity to think and respect the truth.

In a spontaneous way, Ms D described how she feels these things are connected with how she was brought up. In particular, she described her father as a tyrant who needlessly criticized her, and her mother as "weak". One could see how Ms D might have internalized something of the parents' relationship with each other, as well as towards herself.

This was a moving encounter. At the beginning, I had anticipated something different. As the consultation went on, I was especially impressed by Ms D's responses to being understood. This was not simply a matter of her feeling relief, nor of my own sense of being able to think with her. It was also that she could respond insightfully when I pointed out her manoeuvres either to take control or to start moving around dispensing criticism within her own mind.

At the follow-up interview, Ms D expressed how valuable our previous meeting had been. She had felt "lighter", albeit sad, since the consultation, which had been intense and moving for her. She felt she could really use treatment to develop. The detail of what she conveyed accorded with my memory of what had happened. Ms D had clearly thought a lot about our meeting since that first interview.

Working over takes time. The process of changing within a consultation, and between that first interview and a follow-up meeting, gives some indication of how far development may be possible for a given patient. In the following vignette, we see how it may also reveal that the chances of development are slim.

Case vignette: Mr E

Mr E filled out his questionnaire in very neat, condensed writing. He wrote of himself as a child with anxiety and obsessive compulsive disorder, and he described his chronic depression. He detailed his previous unhelpful contacts with doctors. He wrote of his terrible frustration that he has not completed projects on which he embarked years ago.

Mr E arrived on time. He appeared in the lift as a tall, somewhat frail man. He looked at me directly and gave me a firm handshake.

He looked at me blankly and asked what I wanted him to say. I took up how he asks me what *I* want him to say. He shifted slightly. Then he looked at me steadily and quietly. I asked him what was going through his mind. He said he felt "unnerved" by my staring at him. Unusually, however, it was very difficult to pick up quite what this meant for him emotionally, since he continued to look at me without overt indication that he was persecuted or especially anxious.

I therefore said something further about how it remains unclear what he feels he comes for, and what *he* might wish to speak about. In a rather blank way, he said that he wants to get rid of his depression. Sometimes for days he can feel totally lacking in energy. It can be an effort for him just to go to the bathroom or get his food. Then on other days, things are not so bad. He has kept a record of his bad days, and perhaps I would like to see it.

Rather than responding to this invitation, I asked Mr E to say a bit more about how it feels in what he called his "depressions". I also wondered about his feelings about coming here today, given the several psychiatrists and psychologists he has seen before. It might be obvious from this description that already I was feeling more distanced from Mr E than from many of the other patients I have described. It was not that I had given up on him, but I was tentative in nudging matters forward.

Mr E told how, on his bad days, he cannot concentrate on anything. He simply feels lethargic. He said how most of his contacts with professionals were short-lived, mostly "assessments", no real treatment came with them, perhaps they were stepping-stones on the way to the Tavistock Clinic. Coming here, he simply "hoped" that perhaps something would be done about his depression.

I pressed him, that perhaps he might have other feelings about coming, given that nothing has helped him so far. Reluctantly, he conceded that perhaps he thought he might have reached a "dead end". He said it has been a bit like him opening door after door, but they each lead to an empty room.

I took up these two images with Mr E. I commented on how he had to go on hoping, but he feels himself confronted with a "dead end". He has to sustain his hope by opening successive doors, yet again and again these open out onto emptiness. I said it was so difficult for him to feel listened to, properly understood, his problems grasped, and his need for help to be satisfied. He agreed with this.

Making heavy weather, I more or less prompted Mr E to consider how his descriptions seem to reflect his experiences in life. He told of how he was a "loner" as a child, although he did have some friends. He likes to collect things like rocks or shrapnel from the war or other items—he referred to these as "ossified". Now he doesn't socialize and has just one or two friends.

When I took up how his account of childhood was itself skeletal, with no reference to a mother or father, places he lived, school, and so on (I couched this in terms of his description, but was also referring to his manner of relating to me), Mr E spoke of tragic conditions in his family which I shall not describe and conveyed a very difficult childhood. Yet still I felt we were making slow progress, with scant emotional contact between Mr E and myself. I asked whether he dreams.

He replied that he does. I asked for a dream. Initially, he told me of a dream in which *he entered a church, and the rooms kept taking different shapes*. His description of the dream was as spare as the dream itself, and I was left wondering about the qualities (if there were any) to the inside of this church. In another dream, *he had taken a long route round in the countryside at night, finally to arrive at a cathedral. He went inside, and there were large spaces with a great vault*. That was more or less all he described.

I took up the seeming emptiness of the buildings, and he said, yes, there are not many people in this dream. It struck me how the dreams and their telling left the two of us in empty space.

As the consultation drew to its conclusion, I tried to take up that what Mr E calls his depressions appear to be times when he feels that no energy infuses his life, he cannot connect with the emotional meaning of his half-finished projects, and he feels sapped. What he feels left with is something ossified. I said that what he had described of his childhood meant he must have had painful and upsetting times. Yes, he replied, but what is the point of being in touch with pain? I acknowledged that he has kept a delicate balance throughout his life. He said he knows he is inclined to "sweep things under the carpet".

This was a sad and poignant meeting. Mr E's images and dreams provided vivid expressions of his emotional world. There was little to indicate he had the ability or motivation to change, and I was left wondering just how much anguish and pain was ossified within the unyielding structures of his mind.

I conclude this chapter with a vignette that again focuses on seeking activity and vigour as well as the potential for commitment and truth, even in the midst of helplessness and near defeat.

Case vignette: Ms F

Ms F, a woman in her thirties, arrived on time. She appeared composed when I greeted her. Once in the interview room, she flushed and faltered as she began to say why she had come. In a rather organized and articulate manner, she said there are two reasons: first, she has difficulty in consulting with doctors and dealing with a chronic physical disorder, both on a practical level and emotionally. She keeps imagining that she might have illnesses or die overnight of a heart attack, and she has restless nights and ruminations over this. Second, she has had difficulty dealing with relationships and becomes irritable with her businessman partner.

Ms F conveyed that there was a distressing discrepancy between her ability to talk about her problems on the one hand, and a feeling of being out of control in relation to her anxieties on the other.

Very gradually there emerged a rather different side to Ms F. For example, she described how her physical condition began in adolescence, and for two years she was suffering the symptoms and had an idea that something was wrong but did not say anything about this openly to her friends, nor did she consult a doctor. Second, she described how she smokes and can enter a state where she just lives for the moment—clearly implying that she shuts out reality and blocks out influences from outside. Third, she said something more about her anxieties—namely, that she imagines that if she finds out about her state, a doctor might tell her that something is really wrong, and she prefers to live in a state of not-knowing, even though this troubles her deeply.

Something else became clarified by the exchanges between Ms F and myself. On the one hand she managed to describe a lot of important things about herself. At the same time, there was a sense that she kept control within the orbit of her own thinking and explanations about herself. When I made any remark, she tended to say "yes" with a dropping voice, look away, and then pick up on the content of what I had said, now incorporated in a pattern of thinking already familiar to herself. This left Ms F unaffected.

This pattern of relatedness, and its role in maintaining Ms F's emotional equilibrium, became the focus of the interview. I took up how she becomes isolated in her own circular ways of thinking. So, too, she finds it difficult to allow others access to herself in a way that might make a difference. She can actively resist others entering her emotional life in a way that might disturb her. For her to give herself over to a physician (such as myself), who might be able to pin down some problem that is out of her control, would be too great a threat for her. It was evident that she realized that these were matters of huge significance for her.

Then other parts of the picture came into view. There is a determined side to Ms F. If she wants to smoke, she can shut out other considerations. When she feels so inclined, she can use her ruminative thinking to wall herself off from unpalatable sides of herself. I said that she presents herself as a vulnerable person, one who is in need of help, but at the same time she keeps control of what she thinks and feels. I also commented on what seemed like warring factions within her, where she can feel vulnerable and distressed, yet there seem to be parts of her determined to resist or deny those aspects of reality (including her physical condition, but also of a personal kind) that she might feel as intruding upon her well-being.

She seemed to register these ideas intellectually. But as I took them up with her, mostly she managed to defuse their emotional impact by "free-associating". In so doing, she imported the issues back within her own familiar territory. She also responded to some of my remarks defensively, as if they were criticisms, and could feel hurt and not fully understood. The irritability contained in these feeling was disguised, but was present nevertheless.

However, working over can bring change. After a period in which I followed and remarked upon these shifts in what occurred between us, the atmosphere altered. For the last quarter of the interview, Ms F became more emotionally available, much less controlled and controlling, and impressively insightful in ways that I had not entirely expected. She expressed relief that I had picked up her own resourcefulness and capacities, while at the same time pointing out to her how those were deployed so that when she needs determination and courage to face things, she finds she pushes things away.

At the beginning of the interview, Ms F had mentioned that she has recurrent nightmares. I asked her if she could tell me a dream. She told me of one in which *she travelled to a foreign country. She arrived in this complex that was really beautiful with wonderful views, but instead of staying there, she and her companions went to a ramshackle place where there was no running water, the loo had a plant in it rather than being a proper loo, and the beds were distributed in an unsatisfactory way.* Although she sensed meaning in the dream, it really held no insight for her. She seemed to register more when I pointed out some simple things about her situation as depicted, including her need for a functioning loo to flush away some of her less nice feelings, her feeling that she came to take up lodgings that were far inferior to the beautiful lodgings nearby, and the fact that there was no proper place for an appropriate bed. Although it was not possible to work further on the dreams' meanings, I felt hopeful that such work would be fruitful.

I did not attempt to delve further into Ms F's family history, because I considered we had managed to pinpoint some of the most important emotional issues. I suggested we would need to meet once more to discuss possible options. Rather directly, she said it would be important for her to have a psychotherapist who would deal with her "bullshit". When she spoke of her feelings about previous psychotherapists, she conveyed how she had found them supportive and generally helpful but had not felt that they really got hold of her.

Final thoughts

I hope that these vignettes capture the intensity and moving quality of assessment consultations. It is a privilege to meet with people who allow one to enter their emotional worlds in such an intimate manner. A therapist needs to take his or her role very seriously.

Not surprisingly, I am always a bit tense before assessment consultations. I need time to prepare myself mentally. When I was describing consultations in chapter 1, I used the metaphor of falling into a turbulent river. One needs to keep one's bearings even as one becomes caught in currents that threaten to undermine one's professional footing and sweep one away. The positive side is that wherever there is life, there is movement and the possibility of change. So much of a consultation is occupied with locating and freeing up the sources of life and development—well, at least for patients who are not disturbed. With those who are more troubled, as I have indicated, the task can be different.

In the next chapter we consider how to conclude a consultation.

CHAPTER 6

The close

R. Peter Hobson

I have entitled this chapter "The close", but it is not a great title, for only rarely does the close of a preliminary consultation signal the end of the therapist–patient relationship. Often there are follow-up interviews, and therapist and patient may come to have a lengthy history of intermittent contact. More fundamentally, as T. S. Eliot wrote, "In my end is my beginning". The close is also an opening to the future, whatever that may hold.

In this chapter, I shall not confine what I say to describing the final part of a consultation, even though this will be my point of orientation. I would like to illustrate how the conclusion gathers up and develops what has gone before and, at the same time, anticipates and shapes what is to come. I also review the limitations of what can be covered, and what achieved, in the course of a consultation.

Perhaps I should begin by sketching the final quarter hour or so of my consultations. The transition into this phase of the interview is marked by my asking for a dream. When I say, "Can you tell me a dream?", almost invariably the response this elicits is a dismayed "*Any* dream?" I say, yes—any dream. My aim is both to see whether the dream and its telling illuminates what has been happening in the session, and to explore whether or not the patient feels that his or her dream(s) hold meaning. I have already illustrated in several of my case vignettes how I think about and take up dreams (see also R. P. Hobson, 1985).

This exchange provides a stepping-stone to my next enquiry— namely, how the patient has found this meeting. Sometimes I ask what the patient thinks of me. Not always do I take the reply at face value, especially if this is polite. I really do want to discover more about the patient's perspective and about how my experience of what happened dovetails or contrasts with what he or she feels. Beyond this, I can evaluate how forthrightly the patient communicates with myself, and the patient's stance towards his or her own experiences. This stance might well be changing as the consultation heads towards its close.

Sometimes one finds that the depth of interpersonal contact achieved in the session carries through to the end. When this happens, it can be a moving experience as therapist and patient revisit anxieties and other feelings prompted in the opening minutes of the session, now in an atmosphere of mutual respect. Sometimes a patient seems to revert back to a more defensive state of mind, and I have felt disappointment and dismay that what I thought had been established is so easily lost. Sometimes, of course, a patient who has not been able to engage with myself and what I have been trying to do may express frustration and incomprehension and demand onward referral.

When necessary, I make time for a formal review of the patient's psychiatric history and current mental state. It has been rare that I have felt the need to make systematic enquiry about symptoms of, say, biological depression or psychotic experiences or organic impairments in cognitive function. Disorders such as these tend to become manifest early in a consultation, and they prompt an abrupt change in diagnostic tack. However, it is not uncommon to seek specific evidence about a person's suicidal risk, or family history of psychiatric illness, or environmental factors such as social support that may bear upon management decisions.

To conclude, the patient and I address what the consultation has led each of us to believe about the appropriateness of psychoanalytic psychotherapy, or perhaps some alternative approach (which I may need to describe), for the patient. The discussion can be wide-ranging, but the core issues are relatively few in number. What does the person hope to achieve, and is psychoanalytic psychotherapy (whether individual, group, or family treatment, and whether with a trainee or experienced therapist) relevant and appropriate for these aims? Does the patient feel that the approach is meaningful? Is the patient going to be motivated and able to use psychotherapy to develop? Will the process involve significant risk of making the patient's difficulties worse? Are the patient's life circumstances and relationships going to support or undermine treatment, and do they need to be adjusted (e.g., by arranging psychiatric back-up)? Overall, is this really the best form of treatment for this person, and is this the optimal time and place for psychotherapy to take place?

There are, of course, potentially complex aspects to each of these questions. For instance, it is not enough for a patient to be motivated to get better, nor quite enough if he or she is simply eager to change. If psychoanalytic psychotherapy is going to be helpful, the patient needs a grip on, and commitment to, the *kind* of process that is going to be involved if his or her personal development is to be fostered. Expressed thus, this seems like a requirement, a test the patient needs to past. Not surprisingly, patients can feel that this is exactly what it is. But from another perspective, it is an expression of respect for what will or will not make sense for this particular person.

Often, the resolution of what to do next is best left to a follow-up meeting, when both therapist and patient have had a chance to think and to consult others. Follow-up sessions are especially valuable in creating an opportunity to see whether the patient has been able to retain and build on his or her experience. They also allow the patient a chance to express his or her feelings about the initial meeting. Whether such experience was negative or positive, it can be very worthwhile for patient and therapist to acknowledge what the first session had meant.

I end the consultation by asking if there is anything else the patient wants to say. Then I say it is time; I stand up, and I offer to shake the patient's hand. This represents a way of handing back all the patient has given of him/herself over the previous 90 minutes. It marks the transition out of the consulting room and into everyday life.

Once the patient has left, I make sure the door is closed and then take off my tie. I look out of the window. Sometimes I pace around the room for a couple of minutes. Then I reach for my dictating machine.

It is time for a clinical example. I have selected my first vignette to illustrate how the "close" of a consultation may spill over. It always does, in one way or another, but not usually in such a graphic manner. The vignette also highlights ethical issues that arise when one puts someone through a difficult and potentially destabilizing consultation.

Case vignette: Mr G

Mr G was a man referred for anxiety and depression. He arrived on time, casually dressed and conveying a tentative air.

Once in the consulting room, Mr G asked me if I could give him a "plan" as to what was going to happen this morning. I said that the first thing he does is to ask me for my plan of what is to happen (my aim being to prompt us both to reflect on the significance of this opening move). Mr G nodded, paused, and began to look around the room, inspecting the pictures and objects around him. I commented on this. He said he was just finding out where he is. I said how this might also be true in relation to my remark on his request for a plan: when he said he was just "looking around", it seemed that that is not all that is going on. He said yes, but he was not meaning to be obstructive.

What ensued was a period of about 20 minutes in which I devoted great attention to Mr G's seeming unawareness of, and inability to convey, what he was feeling. What characterized this phase of our meeting was that Mr G would downplay any reaction to my comments about his uncommunicative state, and he would reflect (unconvincingly) on how he could see the relevance of all this for other things in his life, how he felt a bit uncomfortable, but how, in all, he felt uncertain what to do and where to progress.

Only very gradually did Mr G come to say more about what he "supposed" he felt at the beginning, and, when pressed, he turned this into what he thought was happening. But not until the end of the interview was he able and prepared to convey more directly how he had a visceral reaction to the way he felt he was being treated. He also referred to his fear and, perhaps most prominently, his need to find out what I wanted so that he did not get turned away from here.

Of course, these anxieties were of great personal significance. However, the major part of the consultation was devoted to addressing how, minute by minute, Mr G would take the life and immediacy out of things he felt or thought, specifically in relation to myself, by "thinking about" such things in a particular way. Initially, Mr G had been unforthcoming, then he tended to speak in abstract ways—for example, "that sounds like the kind of thing I need to address". At other times, he put into a passive voice as happenings what he might have expressed as an active person. When I took up these things with him, he could acknowledge the truth and significance of what I was saying. But I saw no inkling that Mr G might commit himself to do something about it. As I confronted him with this, I could feel him neither with nor against me.

I asked Mr G whether he dreams. He told of a dream in which *he was enhancing the strength of a blue-tack representation of a person.* I asked him if he saw anything significant in this. He laughed and said it was relevant for what emerged today. I said how, in the dream, it was his hands moulding the blue-tack in order to make himself appear a more potent man. He did not seem to be *discovering* the source of vitality and energy in himself.

What happened after the session was that Mr G's son-in-law telephoned the department to say that relatives were unhappy with the degree of disturbance stirred up in Mr G. When I received a message that this had happened, I felt troubled. In part, this was because I might have been facing an official complaint. In part, I was concerned that I might have stirred up difficult feelings that were more than Mr G could manage. At the same time, I was hopeful that the interview might have made something accessible for future work.

Mr G arrived on time for his follow-up meeting. I said how our previous meeting had affected him deeply. He said, yes— what most affected him was how he was "surprised" and not prepared for what happened. He expected something more like questions and answers. It had left him "discombobulated", and he hardly slept that night. He had had fantasies of confronting me.

I acknowledged how, when again he was being very polite, he was, in his way, confronting me with just how unpleasant his experience was, and how he felt that I had jumped on him in a manner that might have been avoidable. Not only was he unprepared, but then, having stirred up his feelings, I told him to leave. He, his son-in-law, and his daughter had to deal with the aftermath. I was explicit that I was unhappy that it had caused him such distress.

Yet Mr G also said he realized that what I had stirred were not so much things that I "made" him feel, but issues with which he was already familiar. Second, he made an insightful remark about a play-off between, on the one hand, his usual ways of coping and, on the other, finding a life. He was also aware that he was allowing his son-in-law to do something on his behalf in phoning the clinic.

I stressed how Mr G keeps his defences in place for a reason. I said we could see how troubled and disturbed he can become. Yet I think he also saw how his "being prepared" and controlling what he expresses, and what he allows to happen, carries a high price.

Mr G entered brief psychotherapy, which came to a premature and largely inconsequential end.

I was disappointed but not surprised at this outcome. I think it was appropriate to explore whether psychotherapy might have enabled Mr G to tap into what was not far beneath the surface. On the other hand, it would have been remarkable had Mr G come to assume a more determined stance in relation to his own passivity. This is especially the case, given that neither I nor his psychotherapist could make much headway in determining the sources and pay-offs of his relational style, nor locate the more aggressive and assertive parts to his personality.

The crunch

It is all very well when therapist and patient arrive at agreement over the outcome of a consultation. Even if the interview has been choppy, and the decision is not to proceed with psychoanalytic psychotherapy, it is often possible to come to a shared view of what has taken place, and why psychotherapy would probably not be helpful.

Nearly always, I feel it is possible to be direct and candid with a patient about the reasons why, in my professional opinion, it is not in his or her best interests to embark on this form of treatment. For instance, if the patient is very troubled, I talk about the threat that psychotherapy can pose. I might express respect for the patient's own ways of dealing with conflicts and anxieties, and I stress that sometimes, in challenging these emotional strategies, psychotherapy can do more harm than good. Or again, if the patient finds the experience of the consultation bewildering or irrelevant, it may be possible to show how this means that treatment is likely to be unfruitful.

Having said this, a therapist is saying "Not here, not this". It is hard to communicate something so disappointing or otherwise negative to someone. The patient has come with a need, along with an idea of how that need may be met. Many patients receive the news that they are not being offered the treatment they sought as a rejection, and rejection is at least unpleasant, sometimes traumatic. Then comes the patient's response, often a mixture of appeal ("What am I supposed to do or say to be accepted?") and aggression ("If you had behaved differently at the start . . .").

To be sure, one might try to soften the blow in several ways—for instance, referring the patient elsewhere, or stating that the person can have a second opinion, or pointing out that the person can return in a year's time for a review (something that, by the way, is often appropriate). But the difficulty remains. And there is no escaping it: it is the therapist's job to say "no" if in the therapist's opinion more harm than good—or perhaps no good at all—would come from saying "yes".

There are other issues that arise if a patient is not offered psychoanalytic psychotherapy. Among the most important are those pertaining to patient choice and to onward referral. These relate to something I discussed earlier—namely, the importance of respecting and standing up for truth.

I believe that, however difficult this might be, a therapist should be as truthful as possible. This does not mean the therapist has to say everything he or she thinks is true, because some things are best left unsaid (something that is proving increasingly problematic for clinicians who fear litigation). What it does mean is that the psychotherapist should not forsake the nature and implications of what he or she has experienced with the patient.

Let me give an example. I have remarked that it is not unusual for patients to come to a consultation with the desire to get rid of some part of their mental life or personality. The unwanted part may be couched in conventional psychiatric terms, such as depression or anxiety, or it may be expressed in terms of the person's difficulties with work, with relationships, or with his or her ill-functioning body. It is also not unusual for these complaints to become transfigured over the course of a consultation. As they appear to the therapist and/or as they are experienced by the patient, the complaints alter in meaning, at least to some degree. They become recognizable as expressions of the person's means to defend against more everyday, essentially non-pathological, conflict and pain. More important still, they are seen to represent facets of the patient's personality and to contain valuable and much-needed as well as problematic content. For instance, a person might devote so much energy to sustaining a particular view of him/herself, or to keeping relationships under tight control, that too little remains to invest in the satisfying things of life. This energy needs to be released and put to better use.

Now, even if there have been moments during the consultation when therapist and patient appear to have converged on insights of this kind, the patient may revert back to his or her original stance, especially as the end of the consultation approaches. For some patients, even this much is elusive, and they find the therapist obtuse, the process without interest or value, and the time of the consultation ill-spent. In such cases, what does one do when the person asks to be referred for another treatment that either implicitly or explicitly entails the view that, yes, the patient is correct in identifying his or her problem as symptoms of a disorder that needs to be eliminated?

The dilemma is whether, in making such a referral, the therapist is colluding with a set of beliefs and procedures which for this patient may reinforce an unsatisfactory status quo, rather than tilting the odds towards development and reintegration. Perhaps just as important, the therapist will seem to be agreeing that what has emerged in the consultation can be set to one side. The tacit message is that it really doesn't matter, after all. On the other hand, if the therapist does not make such a referral, then is he or she disrespectful of patient choice and arrogantly supposing that *only* psychodynamic psychotherapy is relevant for tackling the patient's complaints?

The dilemma is not insuperable, and the therapist has several options. For instance, the therapist might refer the patient back to the original source of referral, and thereby hand back the process of negotiating whether to refer on. Sometimes it is appropriate to refer on oneself. Having said this, I do think such forms of handing-over need to be achieved in a certain way. As a therapist, I hold fast to my view of what has happened in the session and what I take the implications of those happenings to be for the patient's emotional life. I do not push my view, and I stress that the choice of seeking some other means to deal with symptoms must lie with the patient. I express respect for alternative therapeutic approaches. At the same time, I point out that these may not address specific matters that have arisen here and also appear to be important for the patient's difficulties.

If, as a therapist, one has encountered strong, explicit evidence for facts of the matter that have relevance for the patient's emotional conduct and difficulties, then to pretend this is not the case is to abdicate a responsibility—namely, to hold to the truth. Of course it is not appropriate to assault an unreceptive patient with such facts. Besides, one might be wrong. On the other hand, one needs to be someone who can be experienced as seeking after truth, respectful of clinical evidence (which I believe one should be able to pinpoint for the patient, as necessary), and committed to maintaining this disciplined orientation. The patient may or may not recruit a truth-seeking part of him/herself to align with such an orientation, but this approach will give the patient the best chance to do so, either now or in the future.

There are many other important issues about ending not dealt with here, as they are touched on elsewhere in this volume. These include the complexities of referring on to other clinicians (whether or not psychoanalytic psychotherapists) and advising and liaising with other agencies involved in a patient's care. Instead, I am going to state that when all is said and done, it can be very difficult to know how much a patient is going to be able to benefit from psychotherapy. In fact, even after the therapy is over, it is sometimes difficult to know how much a patient has benefitted. My next vignette presents a stretched-out view of several consultations, each with its own close, to illustrate the point.

Case vignette: Ms H

Ms H was a married middle-aged woman who was referred with depression and lack of confidence.

Ms H arrived just over 5 minutes late. As she emerged from the lift she looked at me directly with eyes that were at once smiling and depressed and with an appearance that was at once youthful but ageing.

Once in the interview room, she gave me a quick look and then invited me to explain how psychotherapy is different from counselling (I did not explain). She also wanted me to confirm that this is just a one-off consultation (which I confirmed). This was not a spikey communication. She was trying to get a handle on a difficult situation.

Ms H explained that she has a great deal to cope with. At the same time, she said, it is very important for her to exert control. If she just started talking, it might be the end of the interview already, and that wouldn't do. She also made reference to the danger of things untangling and of her losing everything.

I shall skip over the middle section of the consultation, except to say that Ms H found it difficult to take in things. I tried to illustrate to her how when I said things, she would react, but often to one side and starting from her own stance, so that it rarely felt like we were addressing things together. At one point, she took this as a criticism, that perhaps I was saying that she is hopeless at connecting with people. But I think she understood what I was trying to say.

I asked Ms H whether she could tell me a dream. She said that she never remembers them. She had one yesterday: it was something about it being her job to deliver cartons, perhaps something to do with a train, but she was unable to do this—and then she felt that it was not her responsibility and she felt relieved. Again, it was possible to achieve only half-linkage with her difficulties in really delivering aspects of herself to the interview today. The dream was self-representing, in that it contained a picture of its own unconsummated communication. The dream seemed pregnant with meaning, depicting as it did a difficulty in "delivering" that was connected with Ms H feeling relief when she no longer needed to feel responsible. Yet this meaning never hit home, a missed opportunity for which no one could be held to account.

At the conclusion of the interview, I was explicit that I was unsure what Ms H really wanted for herself. I said I found it difficult to tell how much she was able to make space herself for the issues that matter most. I also expressed concern about the degree to which she was able to allow someone to connect directly with her over these things.

At a follow-up meeting, Ms H arrived on time. She said that she had felt "perplexed" after our last meeting, which she felt was "confrontational". Her principal focus was on the way in which she treads a fine line. She does not want sympathy: she feels the need to change in her way of dealing with things.

I took up with Ms H that if I attempted to be more challenging towards her, she could feel hurt, put down, and not properly appreciated. She can feel that she has tried all she possibly can, and there is no way through. Alternatively, she can begin to "lecture" herself about how she must face the facts of life—nobody can change those. I think she recognized these portrayals. Indeed, as I noted, Ms H could also be attentive and thoughtful in listening to some of my remarks, and there was a sense of her wanting to understand herself.

At a subsequent meeting, Ms H described how in relation to myself she felt mildly misunderstood or got at and somewhat impatient and hurt that I seemed not to grasp her difficulties. At the conclusion of our last meeting, she felt I was a bit "belligerent" but did listen to her and was perceptive.

Ms H joined a group. It was said that initially she engaged well, but she "suffered quite considerable disappointment" when she felt the group "to be unable or unwilling to respond adequately". Eventually she became angry with the group, which she felt was not helping her, and felt let down. She said the group had "got under her skin—but not in a good way".

Subsequently she requested a review with myself. Here she conveyed how she still feels strongly that there is a difficulty in her achieving real fulfilment in her life.

I tried to address with Ms H how, both towards myself and in relation to her life more generally, she seems to find difficulty in allowing herself to be open to others and to receive openly. Instead, she puts things "on the shelf" so that they can be thought about distantly, but not affect her too closely. She also appeared to be anxious that she can seize on things, and turn on herself in a very negative way. In my own experience of Ms H in the countertransference, I felt I had to be careful over what I said. I anticipated (and sometimes received) indication that either she was not quite understood or rather hurt.

In a subsequent meeting, Ms H said she had found our last meeting difficult. She referred to how, outside work, she does not think very much, but goes round and round. As she began to describe this, she slipped into a way of talking about what she already knew about herself. The result was that Ms H wasted time in the session itself and drew away from something more immediate and emotional. On the other hand, I was able to remark on those moments—and in this meeting there were several—when she became quiet and felt understood, rather than blamed. Even here, she would soon shift to say, for instance, that there is "no architecture" to contain her.

In the countertransference, it was possible to feel both the threat of incipient blame or being useless and the potential for true meeting. It transpired that Ms H had looked me up on Google, and it was clear she had felt some serious contact with me.

It is fitting to leave the story in this suspended, and largely but not wholly unconsummated, state. This represents what psychotherapy was able to do for Ms H, and what she was able to make of psychotherapy. This was also the outcome of a lengthy consultation process.

What is missing?

Perhaps it is worth noting what I do *not* do in concluding a consultation. I do not give patients a written formulation. I am aware that offering a formulation is common practice in some forms of psychodynamic consultation, and that some patients have found this valuable.

My reasons for not working in this way are several. First, I take it that everything in a consultation is negotiated. The patient always has the chance to doubt, to disagree, to question, to complain, to object, to express confusion, or to communicate any manner of attitudes towards myself and what I might have said or conveyed. Negotiation of this kind is dynamic and unfolds over time. Most importantly, it is reciprocal. An interpretation is an element within, as well as a focus for, interpersonal dialogue.

But surely, one might object, a written formulation is co-constructed by patient and therapist. Yes, but it renders static what is fluid. In objectifying whatever content is formulated, a formulation is likely to deflect from, as well as distance, a person's experience of intersubjective engagement with the therapist. The very procedure of a therapist coming alongside a patient to discuss what is, in effect, a "diagnosis", lends weight to a certain way of viewing the point of the consultation. It is rather like those times when a therapist and a patient dwell on the patient's history as a record of facts or experiences viewed from a distance, and this serves to deflect from something more immediate and unsafe in the relationship.

A critical question is: Does producing a formulation distil or dissipate, and deepen or skim over, either party's knowledge and understanding of the person to whom the formulation is supposed to apply? Another is: What authority is being given to an oversimplifying as well as cognitively structured text? One can also ask: How *true* is a formulation, and what will the patient make of it over the coming weeks and months?

Perhaps I am ducking something. This is that, as a patient, I know I would hate to be given a formulation. To be formulated, whether or not I had a part in the formulating process, is not what I had come for. If there are rational and civilized reasons for giving a formulation—and certainly there are—I would offset these with something captured by T. S. Eliot's J. Alfred Prufrock: "And when I am formulated, sprawling on a pin, / When I am pinned and wriggling on the wall, / Then how should I begin / To spit out all the butt-ends of my days and ways?"

If this seems too personal a view, then let me throw in a final thought about the generalizations that often feature in formulations, whether or not these are presented to patients. One of the traditional requirements for trainee psychiatrists is that they should be able to make a psychodynamic formulation. Of course it is vitally important that clinicians should think about patients in depth and in developmental perspective. We need to appraise a person's levels of psychological functioning and specify in some detail how the person manages his or her emotional life. Beyond this, however, I am not sure about the value of an abstract and often speculative formulation. Except in specific circumstances when it may be appropriate to refer in a broad-brush manner to classes of patient as (say) "borderline" or "perverse", I would have thought that the best way to capture something of the individual person is to give a small but detailed portrait of the way the person relates to a therapist in a consultation.

At this point, however, I should qualify what I have just written. If formulating ensures that a therapist thinks more systematically about the *range* of factors that may be important for understanding a patient, then all to the good. In particular, a therapist should be able to set a relatively succinct description of what happens within the consulting room in the context of a person's current and past relationships, as well as taking biological and social considerations into account. Psychoanalytic psychotherapy belongs within a bio-psycho-social framework. We forget that at our peril.

This need to review the "whole picture" relates to a different, more specifically psychodynamic reason for considering the question: What is missing? If a psychotherapist does not give due weight to what is missing from the picture that emerges in a consultation, then he or she can mistake a patient's difficulties. What is missing may take the form of a sense of lively engagement, or references to important relationships, or expressions of certain feelings. I am ever alert for the passive male patient with no sign of aggression, or the person whose emotional life seems bereft of subtlety or softness, or especially someone who lies. It may be a capacity to think that seems deficient, or any creative and fulfilling occupation, or some other vital ingredient of a rounded life. One needs to ask why this is missing and what does this say for the person's emotional integrity and his or her potential for becoming disturbed and/or resistant to change.

In other cases, as we have seen in previous case vignettes, what is missing can be located and reintegrated into the personality. My final vignette in this chapter provides a further illustration, one in which the connections between the close of a session and what went before are clearly in view.

Case vignette: Ms I

Ms I was a young woman referred for chronic fatigue that had not responded to previous treatments. She had typed out her questionnaire. She wrote how she has difficulties confronting her partner when she disagrees with him, and how she tends to retreat and withdraw when life gets tough.

Ms I arrived on time. As we walked along the corridor, I told her that Dr A would be sitting in. Rather pointedly, she said: "Who is he?" I said he was a trainee, and she seemed to accept this.

Once in the interview room, Ms I's demeanour became much less forthright, then collapsed. With her eyes half turned away and with little sense of personal engagement, she described how she has chronic fatigue syndrome. She can get into this emotional mode, and she does not know why. By this time, her eyes were watering.

She gazed in front of herself silently, as if she had lost her train of thought. When I said this to her, she described how there are "blocks" in her mind, that often she is unable to think. That is why she has come here . . . and she is getting older.

I took up how she both experiences and presents herself as overwhelmed. The chronic fatigue syndrome has come upon her, right now. She conveys how she gets into these emotional states which she does not understand, and she communicates her helplessness in the face of these difficulties.

She commented that that is not all there is to her.

I said I know, because I felt that in the corridor there had been a moment of more direct engagement. But since that point, it has become unclear how much she is able to be in contact with herself, and with myself.

These themes became central to the assessment. On a number of occasions, I challenged whether the way in which Ms I presents herself is entirely beyond her awareness. I said she might know how she conveys she is unaware of what she does. This constrains her engagement and renders both herself and others one-dimensional. I expressed matters this way, for the reason that I felt that, at this point, we *were* both one-dimensional.

On several occasions, I tracked moments when she became more fully herself and *less* one-dimensional. Each time her response was to move away, often to purvey a description of herself as someone who was usually unable to see this or that (the qualification "usually" was significant, an expression of incipient honesty). In one way or another, she seemed to be actively evading direct confrontation with her own reality, both in the session and in her life. In passing, however, she referred to her needing help to face up to things.

In fact, it took considerable effort to bring Ms I closer to facing up to the way in which she does *not* face up to things. Yet step by step, Ms I was able to recognize and acknowledge this. As the consultation progressed, she conveyed her awareness of how she has an active role in keeping difficult feelings at bay. She knew that this constrained her relationships.

Here we can revisit the working-over phase of a consultation. Early in the session, my predominant attitude was to remark on the seriousness and long-standing nature of Ms I's difficulties. Subsequently I was able to point out, on the basis of recurrent and persuasive evidence from our moment-to-moment exchanges, how intermittent those particular difficulties are. I was forthright and firm in asserting that Ms I's description of herself as someone totally without energy and with a "fatigue syndrome" was at best very partial.

We also came to see more clearly where Ms I's sources of energy had been distributed. As might be expected, this insight came from shifts in Ms I's relatedness with myself.

First, there were a number of occasions when Ms I focused on my own utterances, and her need to grasp them. It was as if she spent her time dissecting the syntax and semantics of my sentences. This was at the expense of assimilating and properly understanding what I was attempting to capture and convey. When I drew attention to this, she commented that her previous treatments had given her an intellectual sense of difficulties in her past. From the way she expressed this, it seemed doubtful whether this "intellectual sense" had been very meaningful.

Second, more energetic parts of Ms I emerged from the emotional woodwork. For instance, she described herself as being "stupid" to not be able to grasp things. At this moment, because of the way she conveyed this, I felt that in due course one might gain access to Ms I's largely disowned or redirected, but also much-needed, aggressiveness and assertiveness, not to mention her capacity for judgement (however harsh).

Every so often, when the status quo seemed to rear its one-dimensional head, I stressed how important it was for her both to experience herself as, and to convey herself to myself as, a helpless person who was trying very hard. She needed to be sympathized with, but not demanded-of too much. Thereby, she and I might be fixed in our respective roles, safe but hardly living.

I asked Ms I whether she dreams. She said that she cannot remember her dreams. I pressed her, and she referred in passing to childhood nightmares. Her eyes watered, and she fell silent. I remarked that these, too, were dreams. Again, however, she declined talking about them and said they were emotionally upsetting. If she was being given the chance to seize the moment, and take the risk of open and potentially creative communication, then she was not taking it.

It would have been less stressful for myself as well as for Ms I if we had moved on, but I chose to wait. Then, after a considerable pause, Ms I described a dream from childhood. *She was in the dark, and there were pieces of furniture flying at her.*

I took up how this depicts a terror that she is trying to avoid. She had earlier referred to how she tries to keep herself from collapsing by not thinking and by not addressing things. Now we could see something of the underlying realities. We could also appreciate the energy contained within the frightening mental furniture that she was fending off.

I asked her what she had thought of me. She said that she thought I was "stern", and then she said she had felt relief that I had picked up some things about her that were helpful. I pointed out how this was a description of a certain kind, in which I as a person was kept "thin". I also referred back to how she had asked the question early on, about whether or not I was just doing this as a one-off assessment consultation. She clearly recognized how she limits what happens in her personal relations, and she appreciated my taking up how difficult this makes it for her to access the kind of help and firmness she needs from other people.

I was explicit about my concern that, although I could see how from moment to moment she could come together and get hold of things, yet her willingness and ability—and commitment and courage—to really face things is still open to question.

Initially she said she was grateful that I gave her a follow up appointment "to give her another chance to get hold of these things". I said that no, that was not the point—she had already had the chance to do that today. The issue is now what she does with it, and where she feels this takes her, for the future.

In the follow-up meeting, she arrived on time. She described how at our initial meeting she had felt "overwhelmed by something"—which she then changed to "dug myself into a hole".

I explored these two rather different accounts of herself, and I tried to pinpoint just how much she really believes she plays a role in generating her own states of mind. Although I think she took this seriously, what was more doubtful here and for the rest of the consultation was how far insight gives her a sense of hope, or a grip on her own ways of dealing with things. Rather, in this meeting, it seemed to be linked with a feeling of despair that she fights against. She described how, today, she was like a little child returning, how she feels threatened. In the moment-to-moment interactions in this meeting, however, she seemed defeated by the task of getting hold of this and of moving forward. The prevailing atmosphere was one in which she felt in need of "help".

Ms I entered brief psychoanalytic psychotherapy, a treatment 16 sessions in length. Initially, she found it difficult to express and reflect upon feelings and, indeed, to engage with her psychotherapist in a personal manner. She was anxious about collapsing and not being able to function and anxious about whether she should commit herself to the psychotherapeutic relationship more deeply. When pressed, she would tend to become tearful or go blank or otherwise seem unable to confront difficult issues. At times this left the psychotherapist frustrated and irritated.

Gradually, however, Ms I's own involvement in eliciting distanced and even cruel reactions from others became more explicit. She was able to talk about her difficulties in relating and loving. She came to see, emotionally as well as intellectually, how she would retreat to a hideout where she was protected but isolated. Movingly, she experienced regret about the implications of this stance, and she became more direct and emotionally available as well as assured and insightful as a person.

All this was possible only because her therapist overcame her own anxieties about challenging Ms I's habitual ways of managing her relationships and trusting that Ms I could face the uncertainties of the future. In the end, the therapist felt very touched as well as impressed by Ms I's new-found genuineness, hope, and creativity.

Final thoughts

One function of a consultation is to predict how a person will fare in psychoanalytic psychotherapy. In my view, this is a very uncertain business. One can easily underestimate a person's ability to connect with a psychotherapist who (it may turn out) is "right" for this individual. Therefore, if a patient has a clear enough idea of what is in store, is not going to be harmed by the experience, and wants to engage in psychotherapy, then I need strong grounds for advising that he or she should look elsewhere.

Many a time I have felt very uncertain about a patient's prospects and have been surprised and impressed with what emerged and developed in psychotherapy. Many a time, too, what had seemed real promise for movement and benefit remained unfulfilled. A patient's dogged aversion to change, or, sometimes, well-justified caution about relinquishing a hard-won equilibrium, may become apparent only as treatment unfolds. At the end of the day, we are making informed guesses about an uncertain future.

The question that remains, therefore, is how best to become informed. I shall not go over the many considerations that are relevant for evaluating the potential value or otherwise of psychotherapy for particular patients. One matter does justify further comment, however. How intimate and potentially exposing does a psychoanalytic psychotherapy consultation need to be?

This issue arose earlier, in relation to how best to begin a consultation. I shall not rehearse the arguments here, except to re-state that different psychotherapists need to do what they do best, in the patient's best interests. What I want to consider very briefly is the variety of ways in which choices arise.

For example, one can make a case for asking patients for a sexual fantasy. No doubt, this can be very revealing. I do not do this. It not as a matter of principle—I can imagine myself doing so, if I thought it necessary. Rather, if it is *not* necessary, then I spare the patient this particular form of enquiry at a preliminary meeting.

There are times when I choose to spend relatively little time asking about a patient's early history. True, if this has not been mentioned by the middle of a consultation, I say something like: "How do you think you became the person you are?" But again, if I feel I have learnt enough from other sources, and in particular from the transference and reports of the person's current relationships and emotional life, then enough is enough.

This can be a source of frustration to colleagues when I present my consultations for discussion. Some feel they cannot get to know the patient properly if they are not told about the person's background. Fair enough, but that is partly a personal preference. I consider that my task is to do just as much as is required to see what I need to see, and to engage to the degree it is necessary to engage, in order for both the patient and I to complete the work that is needed for a consultation. There is a time to back off, as well as a time to delve deeper.

Talking of which, in the next chapter I would like to delve deeper into how a psychoanalytic psychotherapist thinks and works.

CHAPTER 7

The minute particulars

R. Peter Hobson

Т he transference is like a shoal of fish. As a therapist peers into the passing stream, hoping to catch a glimpse of distinctive life-forms, all that appear are flashes of reflected sunlight. Then the surface ripples seem to settle. The waters deepen. Moving shapes, sometimes definite shapes, reveal themselves to the feeling eye.

I have said that, in psychotherapy, all is movement. I have stressed the value of following shifts in stance as patient and therapist weave their way through a consultation. Yet my clinical examples have portrayed the to-and-fros from a semi-distanced vantage point. In this chapter, I shall come to take a closer look at how configurations of internal relations are reflected in the minutiae of patient–therapist exchanges.

The chapter is unusual in falling into three sections that contrast in style as well as content. The first section is an exposition of Freud's "Mourning and Melancholia" (1917e [1915]); in the second, I consider different views on what it means to think about and interpret the transference; and the third is a moment-by-moment account of the beginning phase of a consultation. The three sections are united in theme: the value of attending to the minute particulars of a person's clinical presentation and engagement.

Earlier I drew attention to an echo from my father's book, *Forms of Feeling* (R. F. Hobson, 1985). On this occasion, I have lifted wholesale the title he used for the second half of his volume. I trust that, had he been alive, this would have made him smile. He drew on the following quote from William Blake's *Jerusalem*, II, 55, 60–8: "He who would do good to another must do it in Minute Particulars / General Good is the plea of the scoundrel, hypocrite, & flatterer, / For Art & Science cannot exist but in minutely organized Particulars."

I begin by considering how Freud's (1917e [1915]) attentiveness to the minute particulars of a melancholic's presentation led him to discover how internal "object relations" structure emotional experience (see also Ogden, 2002). Here Freud was not especially concerned with moment-by-moment patient–therapist exchanges. Having said this, his sensitivity to subtleties in a patient's stance and relatedness represents exactly the kind of perceptiveness needed for tracing movements in the transference. Besides this, Freud's account of psychopathology in melancholia is directly applicable to the patient I shall come to describe.

"Mourning and Melancholia"

The first few pages of "Mourning and Melancholia" (Freud, 1917e [1915]) represent the very summit of psychoanalytic writing. Freud begins by noting that the views he will propound may not be valid for all cases of melancholia, by which he means very serious, more or less psychotic depression. Then he makes a connection between the depressive state of melancholia and a normal state of mourning, a connection that is not at all obvious. He lists certain distinguishing features of melancholia, several of which are normally shared with mourning:

> a profoundly painful dejection, cessation of interest in the outside world, loss of the capacity to love, inhibition of all activity, and a lowering of the self-regarding feelings to a degree that finds utterance in self-reproaches and self-revilings, and culminates in a delusional expectation of punishment. [p. 244]

If there are important similarities between mourning and melancholia, and mourning is a response to loss, then perhaps serious depression, too, is related to loss. In the case of melancholia, the loss would not necessarily be conscious; it would be reacted to in an extraordinary way, to produce the illness; and the person reacting in such a way might well be predisposed to do so. Freud also highlights the most notable contrast between mourning and melancholia—namely, a marked disturbance in self-regard in the latter:

> In mourning it is the world which has become poor and empty; in melancholia it is the ego itself. The patient represents his ego to us as worthless, incapable of any achievement and morally despicable; he reproaches himself, vilifies himself and expects to be cast out and punished. He abases himself before everyone and commiserates with his own relatives for being connected with anyone so unworthy. [p. 246]

Already Freud does more than describe how a patient thinks and feels. He draws attention to how the patient "represents his ego to us", implying that we need to address the act of communication. What might it mean to represent oneself to other people in this particular way? In addition, Freud highlights the patient's relational activity in reproaching and vilifying himself, as well as the harshness with which he expects to be treated by others. Freud continues:

> It would be equally fruitless from a scientific and a therapeutic point of view to contradict a patient who brings these accusations against his ego. He must surely be right in some way and be describing something that is as it seems to him to be. [p. 246]

Rather than weighing in to suggest how negative cognitions might be corrected, Freud reflects that it must be we, the observers, who have failed to grasp something. Of course we do not know *how* the patient is right, nor why things should seem as they do, but this is the point from which we should embark. So, what does further reflection yield?

> We see how in him one part of the ego sets itself over against the other, judges it critically, and, as it were, takes it as its object. [p. 247]

We had thought we were observing a single, unified individual. But in fact, we are witnessing a *relation* between two quasi-individuals, within the one embodied person. Close examination reveals that one part of the person is locked in a sadomasochistic engagement with another part. The phenomenology of this kind of depression discloses an underlying intrapsychic relation with very unpleasant qualities.

Here Freud has reached a turning-point in psychoanalytic theory, and he presses on with his quest to understand yet more. In particular, he addresses the question of how a person could have become trapped in such an emotional entanglement.

At several points in the paper, Freud exhorts us to *listen*, really listen, to what the patient is saying and how the patient is saying it:

> If one listens patiently to a melancholic's many and various self-accusations, one cannot in the end avoid the impression that the most violent of them are hardly at all applicable to the patient himself, but that with insignificant modifications they do fit someone else, someone whom the patient loves or has loved or should love. . . . So we find the key to the clinical picture: we perceive that the self-reproaches are reproaches against a loved object which have been shifted away from it on to the patient's own ego. [p. 248]

In this way, Freud is suggesting that melancholia may indeed be prompted by the loss of a person, either literally or symbolically. The patient feels hatred as well as attachment to the lost person. With the loss, the ego (or part of the self) becomes identified with the other, so that feelings towards the person are now directed towards the self. The melancholic is at once the attacker and the attacked; in hating himself, he is at the same time hating someone else. Having become identified with the one who is hated, he is now subject to his own derogatory attacks.

> Thus the shadow of the object fell upon the ego, and the latter could henceforth be judged by a special agency, as though it were an object, the forsaken object [i.e. person]. In this way an object-loss was transformed into an ego-loss and the conflict between the ego and the loved person into a cleavage between the critical activity of the ego and the ego as altered by identification. [p. 249]

This is developmental theorizing of a radical kind, in that it traces how a highly ambivalent external relationship can become a highly ambivalent internal relationship. The mechanism of this developmental change is that of identifying with someone else. The outcome for the structure of the mind is an internal world peopled by figures who exist in active relation to one another. These internal relations are not *merely* internal, however, for they can implicate people in the external world. For example, why does the melancholic go on and on talking, if he or she feels so abject? The listener is assailed by some nasty stuff.

Freud proceeds to make a number of further important but subsidiary suggestions. In particular, he proposes that the premelancholic is disposed to this form of illness by the kind of intense ambivalence that characterizes his intimate relationships, as well as by his propensity to react to loss by the kind of identification described.

I trust that this brief excursion into Freud serves a useful purpose in characterizing a set of ideas and attitudes that can inspire anyone conducting therapeutic consultations. Shortly I shall illustrate how these ideas have influenced my own clinical work. Before this, I provide some background to technical aspects of the consultation I shall describe.

Working in the transference

Freud (1912b) was forthright about the need to tackle psychopathology as a patient lives out his patterns of (internal and external) relations as these are realized vis-à-vis the analyst— that is, in the transference. However, there are different ways of working in the transference, and here I offer observations on just a few matters over which contrasts may arise (see also Riesenberg-Malcolm, 1995; Roth, 2001). This should help when it comes to appraising the example of clinical work that follows and should draw attention to different levels of focus that a clinician may adopt in appraising the transference. In addition, the ideas will provide background for the research study on transference interpretations described in chapter 10.

Psychoanalysts and psychoanalytic psychotherapists differ in the emphasis they give to particular features of the transactions that take place between patient and therapist. Some (e.g., Kohon, 1986; Sandler, Holder, Kawenoka, Kennedy, & Neurath, 1969) consider that only certain of the various goings-on in the patient–therapist relationship should be considered as manifestations of transference and countertransference, and they take the view that one should respect the process of "gathering the transference" over time. On the other hand, there are psychoanalysts (exemplified by Joseph, 1985) who, while not wishing to claim that everything that happens in treatment is of a single kind, endorse Klein's (1952) formulation of the "total situation" that a patient transfers into the psychoanalytic relationship. This orientation gives us a picture of "transference as a relationship in which something is all the time going on" (Joseph, 1985, p. 164).

What follows from this for a therapist's interventions and, perhaps especially, his or her activity in interpreting the transference? One of the therapist's aims in giving interpretations is to make explicit otherwise unrecognized aspects of the relationship between patient and therapist. Racker (1968) described the extremes of "the silent analyst", who tends to wait for the opportune moment for interpretation, and the analyst who considers that, in principle and potentially, every moment is opportune, since every moment contains a "point of urgency"—not least, very early in treatment. A given therapist's style of interpreting is likely to correspond with his or her view of what is most significant in the evolving patient–therapist relationship, how long it takes for this to emerge, and how best its meaning might be captured and conveyed.

If they view qualities of immediate interpersonal engagement to be critically important for the therapeutic endeavour, then no wonder that psychoanalysts like Joseph (1985) give special emphasis to movement and change within the transference. Such movements occur in how a patient uses the analyst, not merely what he or she expresses or describes. A psychotherapist's attentiveness to shifts in relatedness yields insight not only into particular feelings or thoughts of which a patient may be unaware, but also into the level of psychic organization on which the patient is functioning and, with this, the nature of his or her anxieties at any given moment.

Then there is a question of how interventions are to be framed. This will depend on how a psychotherapist conceives of the developmental processes that he or she is intending to promote. There are some psychotherapists who would stress that their own role is to offer suggestions, even "hypotheses", about the meaning of a patient's difficulties, in such a way that they are seen to be inviting a mutual exploration of possibilities rather than (they might critically suggest) talking "at" the patient or prescribing the truth. This stance may be contrasted with that of psychotherapists who see the therapeutic action of psychoanalytic psychotherapy to reside more in the kind of processes characterized by Strachey (1934) and Bion (1962), involving an immediate re-enactment of unconscious phantasy in which the therapist is implicated, but which the therapist then transforms through containment and understanding. Here the psychotherapist may be forthright in attempting to formulate what he or she thinks is happening in the relationship, so that the patient experiences the intervention not "from the side" (in alliance with the therapist, reviewing some relevant issue) but from a position within the occurring phantasy.

Such contrasts in perspective may help us to evaluate our own and others' clinical work. When one reads or hears a clinical description, it is easy to assume that what unfolded would have done so more or less whatever a therapist had said or done. It is also easy to suppose that one's own technique corresponds with—though no doubt, somewhat improves on—that which another therapist describes. At times such assumptions and suppositions may be correct. I suspect that more often they are not.

So now I turn to a consultation that illustrates what Freud described in "Mourning and Melancholia", albeit in someone much less disturbed than the patients he had in mind. I shall trace how sadomasochistically coloured patterns of relatedness are apparent not only within the patient, but also between patient and therapist in the transference and countertransference.

Case vignette: Ms J

I am going to describe and discuss the specifics of a series of patient–therapist exchanges that took place at the beginning of an assessment consultation. Mostly, the account is in terms of what the patient said, then what I said, and so on, back and forth. Unusually in this case, I mostly held back from making direct comment on the patient's relations with myself in these early exchanges, choosing instead to prepare the ground for such interpretations. Interpolated between quotations are my understandings of what was happening, and reflections on therapeutic principles exemplified by my interventions.

The reason that I can report the details of what therapist and the patient said to each other is that the beginning phase of the consultation was transcribed. This was a meeting that happened many years ago, when from time to time I would videotape my assessment interviews. In fact, if I recall correctly, this was the very first such interview captured on tape. A shorter version of the following account also appeared in my previous book, *The Cradle of Thought* (Hobson, 2002).

> The patient, Ms J, arrived on time for this first assessment interview. When I offered to shake her hand, which was also captured on videotape (at that time, patients came directly to my room), something odd took place. Somehow—I could not tell how—I felt thrown off balance. It was as if I had been clumsy and had made an awkward gesture. This was not a pleasant experience. But I more or less recovered and then sat down.

> I began the session in my customary way by introducing myself, saying how long we had, and then falling silent. With barely a pause to register what was happening, or what my state of attentiveness might be, Ms J began recounting in a monotone how she didn't know why she got depressed, there didn't seem to be any reason for it,

> ". . . and if I'm feeling OK, when I do anything, I'm the type of person that always likes to have everything perfect. When I feel OK and I do what I have to in the office, no matter what it is . . . well, when I try to tackle anything, if I do, I just feel that it is not the way I want it to be. Do you know what I mean, no?"

> This excerpt represents a distillation of a drawn-out soliloquy. Ms J was speaking almost to herself, with hardly a look towards myself. As she spoke, I found my heart sinking. At the end of this initial statement about herself, Ms J suddenly looked up at

me, then away again. Although in her words she was asking if I knew what she meant, there was little to suggest she was interested in what I might have to say. I felt that perhaps I should say something to show that I was listening and to summarize where I thought we had come thus far.

Struggling for words, I began: "You convey . . ." But before I got any further, Ms J interrupted:

"When, say I have got this filing to do, well, when I feel OK I will do it and although I'm never really satisfied with it, I mean, it's the best I can do. And say my aunt came to see me, I would say to her, I feel everything is a mess, and she would say to me, I'm too fussy. Well, I am, I know myself that when I do something I do it better than most people, I'm more fussy than most people, but I never feel satisfied, and when I get depressed I won't even attempt to do it because I will never get it really in order. That's just the way I feel about everything really."

At this point, there was a pause. By now I felt at a loss. I wanted to say something to help, but I didn't know what that something might be. Ms J herself seemed hopeless about the possibility of receiving help, and I wondered if she felt there was little point in trying to communicate with me. I said:

"And even trying to describe it to me you get quite worried whether you will be able to get it across."

Ms J gave a sighing and distinctly unenthusiastic "Yeah". In response, and with some desperation, I tried to resuscitate my sentence by adding:

"And give enough reasons and give a description that is good enough."

Ms J's response was to ignore what I had said, and to continue as if I had not spoken:

"I suppose in a way I hate myself for being like this, but I can't control it. I don't know what else to say really, it's just that, you know, no matter what I do I'm never satisfied."

There was a long pause. There was little to suggest that Ms J was expecting me to say anything. She appeared to have had her say and was neither anxious about nor interested in what might happen next.

I tried to gather my thoughts. My attempt to offer an understanding remark had seemed a clumsy and useless thing to have done. Here we were, gloomily stuck and with scant prospect of escape from the stuckness.

It occurred to me afterwards how, had I been a primary-care doctor or a busy general psychiatrist, the pull to action would have been irresistible. I would have begun by asking systematic questions about the phenomenology of Ms J's mental state— could she say a bit more about how she felt, were things better or worse in the mornings or evenings, how was her sleep, could she find interest in some things?—and then I would have reached for the prescription pad. It would have been a relief to give Ms J something that might (just might) improve her condition. Perhaps more important, if I prescribed medication, it would have allowed me to show her the door. I would not have had to deal with her oppressive difficulties until a follow-up appointment three weeks later.

Under these circumstances, then, aside from any psychiatric justification that might apply, prescribing medication would have fulfilled a number of emotional needs. First, I would have offered something, and Ms J would have received something. After all, Ms J came in need, and she was expecting help. Second, I would have avoided the immediate prospect of feeling a failure and inadequate in what I could do. Third, I would have deflected awareness away from my own hostility to Ms J. At the same time, I would have expressed that hostility by cutting her off and sending her home with something to "make her better".

Instead, I knew that my job as a psychotherapist was to do my best to survive the next hour and a half sitting with Ms J, as I tried to fathom what was happening and what this might signify. Perhaps most important, I had to hold back from action, insofar as action meant living out the role into which Ms J had inducted me.

My current inaction, then, was not "going silent" on Ms J. I needed to avoid unhelpful action that might interfere with understanding. I needed to think.

Then something struck me. When I had referred to Ms J's anxiety about communication with me, what I had said did not ring true for Ms J at the moment I said it. But it did ring true for what *I* was feeling. *I* was worried whether I would be able to get anything useful across, and *I* felt I would be unable to give enough reasons or give a description that was good enough. Not only did I feel this, I also expressed what I felt in both the delivery and content of my interpretation. By reflecting on what my own behaviour and stance revealed to myself, I came to understand something important about Ms J.

What I had grasped at this point was that someone in this relationship was both anxious and intimidated by the pressure to come up with something worthwhile.

After one or two more stuttering exchanges in which Ms J said she did not know what else to say, I remarked:

"What you convey is that there is something in you that requires nothing less than perfection."

The point of this remark was to take up an issue that Ms J had emphasized. This had seemed important for Ms J's self-criticism, but also something that was relevant to what was happening in relation to myself at that very moment.

It may be worth commenting on some other features of this intervention. What I said took the form of a statement, not a question. I was trying to capture what was happening at the moment I spoke. I had pretty good evidence for what I said in Ms J's repeated assertions about her not being satisfied. This tallied with my countertransference and, specifically, my own trepidation in saying anything. In addition, of course, my statement conveyed that I was listening to and trying to understand what Ms J was communicating. I was setting communication centre-stage.

I had another aim. When someone presents with self-criticism, it is not difficult to sympathize. We tend to identify with the person as criticized. We might want to encourage the person to be more positive about him/herself and to marginalize "negative cognitions". As Freud made clear, however, we need to contend as well with the person as critic. In the case of Ms J, I needed to begin to address how, in a part of herself, she was actively critical and unsatisfied.

So I made my intervention. How did Ms J respond? With a sigh. Ms J resumed her monotone, thus:

"I don't know really, since I was a child I used to, even the likes of getting my things ready for school and that, although my grandmother did them for me I preferred to do it myself because I felt that nobody could do it the way I did it and I think, I don't know whether it started from (*pause*) when I was (*pause*) it used to be just . . . when I was at school I remember that I used to just like everything to be perfect and no one could do it the way I did it, I preferred to do it myself; I think it's just escalated from there."

I said: "So there's something additional. It's not just that you can't do things well enough, but even before that, at school, there was a feeling that nobody else could do things well enough, that only you could approach perfection with your getting ready for school and other things."

Here I was simply trying to recapitulate what Ms J had been saying. Well, not so simply. I was expanding and at the same time clarifying the picture. The expansion was that, from childhood on, Ms J's impatience and severity was directed at anyone who tried to help. The clarification was that she and only she was allowed to do anything—as I was discovering first-hand.

Ms J's reaction to my statement was to sigh again. She conveyed that what I had said was really not worth my breath. Yet at the same time, when *she* resumed her account—that is, when she was doing something rather than I was doing it—she seemed to express very similar ideas:

"Yeah, it was just, . . . it wasn't really at school, it was just, . . . I was just giving you an example of it . . . when I was getting something ready, or if I was going somewhere. Even when I was small I elected to do it myself because I thought no one could do it the way I did it."

By now, I realized that I had to be very careful not to take the lead in anything I said about Ms J. Any insights that I might have would be dismissed rather than thought about. Although there was pressure on me to provide something worthwhile, it was hazardous even to offer ideas. The problem was not so much that I would have to suffer the consequences—that is something for which I am paid. Rather, I would be living out my role in Ms J's script. This would not help her to think, nor move us forward.

Therefore when Ms J returned to the idea that all this might have started when she was small, I steadfastly avoided following her lead.

I said: "You ask me."

Ms J mumbled something.

I said: "I wonder if you have asked yourself."

She said: "Well, I think it did, I think it began . . ."

Trying to secure what seemed to be an important shift towards genuine reflection in Ms J, I pressed the issue home: "I wonder if you yourself really believe . . ."

After hesitation, Ms J said in a convincing and moving way:

"Oh, I supp . . . I think that it's . . . well, when I was small, my grandmother used . . . no matter what I did, it was never right, she used to always . . . well, that's just it in a nutshell. No matter what I did it was never right, or never good enough or nor, I don't know . . . well, it's just that, no matter what I did it was never right. I couldn't do anything right. I suppose it was because I was the oldest, she used to take things out on me. Maybe she didn't even mean . . . she was just dissatisfied with her own life."

It is very unlikely that Ms J had ever had previous contact with a psychotherapist or had read psychoanalytic literature. This last description had the ring of truth about it, and I felt genuine sympathy for Ms J's continuing struggles with herself and her relationships.

Although I do not know what actually happened in Ms J's childhood, I believe that what she described was probably accurate. What I knew first-hand, and therefore with confidence, was the kind of unsatisfied and unsatisfying relationship she was liable to establish with someone else. I realized why previous physicians had become exasperated with their failed attempts to help. The relationship she was living out with me had the very same pattern as the relationship towards herself that she had described right at the start of the interview.

In this vignette, we can see how, in the very first phase of the consultation, something pivotal for Ms J's difficulties is not merely described, but also lived out. We can also trace how what was (probably) an interpersonal configuration of relatedness between a child and her grandmother became an intrapsychic configuration of relatedness within that child's mind. It was still apparent now, within the mind of the child-become-adult. In the therapeutic consultation, the pattern was lived out not only in Ms J's relations with herself, but also in her relations with myself as therapist. Now the *therapist* was having to experience the feelings of this child-cum-adult who struggled to satisfy someone else, but in vain. As the therapist, I also sensed how easily I might find myself, like the doctors before me, in the position of a dominant figure who was unsatisfied and frustrated.

Let me return to that initial handshake. William Blake wrote of seeing a world in a grain of sand. If the first few minutes of a consultation are a grain of sand, then the first 10 seconds are a near-microscopic particle. Yet contained within those first seconds of meeting was a core truth about Ms J.

I went back to the first half-minute of the videotape of the session. What I found there was a behavioural expression of what I had registered as countertransference in my subjective experience. When Ms J came into the room, I had extended my hand as I introduced myself. Ms J responded by reaching forward with her hand.

Then in the instant before our hands met, she withdrew hers just a fraction. It was enough to generate in me a tiny but seismic shock. With remarkable specificity, my feelings at that moment were to map on to the feelings that Ms J was to describe, and have the two of us live out, in the events that were to follow.

Final thoughts

My account of Ms J has contained a mix of verbatim quotations and commentary. Mostly, the commentary has comprised descriptions of, and reflections upon, my countertransference. Here have I tried to capture and convey what I felt in relation to the patient as our interaction unfolded. The aim of my account was not to get feelings off my chest—although sometimes after a session, one does need to find a way to push out feelings that a patient has pushed in—but, rather, to examine how my experience reflected what the patient was enacting in the consultation.

It is a characteristic but inconstant feature of having feelings "projected into" oneself that one feels *both* caught up in having those feelings *and* somehow stirred up and acted-upon. Only partly do the feelings feel one's own. And that is right. In part they belong to oneself, and in part they belong to the patient.

One of the things I felt with Ms J was that the roles could easily be reversed. I registered within myself the impulse to become impatient and dismissive. There may have been moments during the consultation when, despite my best efforts, I partly followed through on that impulse. Very likely I thought thoughts of which I was uneasy and even ashamed. If a patient is being sadistic towards oneself, one is likely to become either masochistic or sadistic in response.

I was self-consciously aware of my restraint and care in modifying my attitudes, in order that I could maintain a stance that was neither attacking nor passively submissive. But it hardly needs saying that such neutrality, insofar as it was achieved, was only one facet of my emotional state. Ms J affected me powerfully.

We psychotherapists lay ourselves open to being communicated with, pushed and pulled, drawn in and kept out, elevated and denigrated, shat into and fed from, and all manner of other things. We do so for a purpose. I had my work cut out relating to my own relations with Ms J, in order both to understand what was happening and to make appropriate interventions.

This is the most detailed account I have given of what intersubjective engagement means. In recounting what happened, it was helpful as well as reassuring to have a verbatim transcript. Yet if you ask me whether I would prefer to supervise a trainee who brings a verbatim transcript, or one who recounts a session in his or her own best efforts to convey a "She said, I said" account, I would go for the latter. Of course such an account is selective. Yet when one combines what is selected with the way the trainee communicates his or her attitudes to the patient—something that is often implicit and is captured in what the trainee reports of the verbal exchanges—then one has a good chance of discerning how the patient is functioning and how the therapist is becoming implicated. I suspect that if in this chapter I had given a spontaneous report of the beginning of the consultation with Ms J, I might have conveyed as much.

SPECIAL DOMAINS

In Part IV we turn to how consultations assume special characteristics, and yield special insights, when they involve patients who have suffered trauma and/or who are especially troubled.

CHAPTER 8

Trauma

Joanne Stubley

My aims in this chapter are twofold. First, I consider how a brief series of consultations might be of value for individuals who present with trauma. Second, I discuss how the psychological effects of trauma yield insights into the workings of the mind. Such insights are relevant for therapeutic work beyond that with traumatized patients.

I begin with a clinical description, but not of someone who came for consultation.

A person's story of trauma

A young college student, walking through a park on the way home from a party, is brutally raped. In the following weeks two other women are attacked in a similar manner, but they lose their lives at the hands of their attacker. The college student experiences post-traumatic stress reactions in the form of nightmares, flashbacks, difficulty sleeping, feelings of isolation and distance from friends and family, emotional numbness, and withdrawal.

Unable to return to classes, the student leaves college and returns home. There she finds it difficult to speak about her experiences. She finds herself embroiled in pointless arguments and disputes within the family. She breaks up with her former boyfriend and sees many of her old friends drift away. Eventually she begins to pick up the pieces of her life, restarting college in another town.

This might have been the end of the story as far as we are concerned. But the young woman was studying creative writing. In time she wrote an autobiographical account of her experiences, called "Lucky". It is a harrowing and at times disturbing narrative (Sebold, 1999). It provides us with a portrait of what this kind of traumatic experience can be like and reveals the impact it may have on a person's life.

Again this might have been the end of the story, except that this woman, Alice Sebold, went on to write a novel she called *The Lovely Bones* (2003). The book opens with Susie, a 14-year-old girl, being raped and murdered in a cornfield. The story is told from the perspective of Susie in heaven, watching over her grief-stricken family and friends as they struggle with the reality of their loss. We come to understand what the trauma meant for the family, against the backcloth of their past and present lives. With incredible intimacy, we are given insight into the thoughts and feelings of the victim, the bereaved, and the murderer.

What is most striking is the life and hope the book holds. One senses the writer's deep understanding of the nature of trauma, loss, and bereavement. She allows us to journey with the characters as they find their own ways of coming to live with such an event in their lives.

The intermediate heaven where Susie goes is complex and deeply interesting, not least in helping us to explore what grieving entails:

> I did begin to wonder what the word heaven meant. I thought, if this was heaven, truly heaven, it would be where my grandparents lived. Where my father's father, my favourite of them all, would lift me up and dance with me. I would feel only joy and have no memory, no cornfield and no grave.
> You can have that, Franny said to me. Plenty of people do.
> How do you make the switch? I asked.

It's not as easy as you might think, she said. You have to stop desiring certain answers.

I don't get it.

If you stop asking why you were killed instead of someone else, stop investigating the vacuum left by your loss, stop wondering what everyone left on earth is feeling, she said, you can be free. Simply put you have to give up on earth.

This seemed impossible to me. [Sebold, 2003, p. 120]

We come to see how, over the years, each member of the family manages his or her own grief. Susie's mother, full of guilt for her own ambivalence when she was pregnant with this first child, leaves the family, embarking on an affair before moving away to live alone and work in a menial job. The younger sister, Lindsey, struggles to make sense of her own life as adolescence takes hold, at times hardening herself to the unbearable reality but slowly finding new attachments and moments of beauty in the world. The youngest child, a boy, finds himself caught between the loss of his sister and then the loss of his mother. As Susie describes it to us:

He dreamed of being Wolverine, who had a skeleton made of the strongest metal in the universe and who could heal from any wound overnight. At the oddest moments he would think about me, miss my voice, wish I would come out of the house and pound on the roof of his fort and demand to be let in. . . . When he felt his heart hurt he turned into something stronger than a little boy, and he grew up this way. A heart that flashed from heart to stone, heart to stone. [p. 217]

Dominant themes

I shall begin by laying out the principal themes of this chapter.

The centrality of meaning

How does one make sense of a traumatic event in the context of one's life? For most of us, our lives are spent knowing that this is the ground we walk on, this is what it means to wake up every morning, to breathe this air, to speak these words, to live this life. Trauma challenges and changes the meaning of all of this.

Among the meanings that a traumatic event has for an individual, those established at an unconscious level are among the most important. Often a person's experience of trauma links up with his or her earlier experiences in life, especially those that have featured in previous relationships.

From a therapeutic point of view, it is vitally important to understand the meaning that has been given to a traumatic event, often on an unconscious level. It allows one to see what has held back recovery, as well as anticipate what may occur in the therapeutic encounter.

The importance of words

In the face of trauma, our capacity to symbolize, and in particular to use words to describe our experiences, thoughts, and feelings, becomes impaired. When words are no longer available, there is a pressure to act. Although action may take many forms, one important push is to repeat the traumatic experience in some form. Freud (1920g) described this as the "repetition-compulsion".

In re-enacting trauma, traumatized patients may identify with various figures and/or elements involved in the traumatic events. This process may determine not only the form of a person's difficulties, but also his or her behaviour in psychoanalytic consultation and treatment.

Loss and mourning

All trauma involves loss, and loss requires one to mourn.

It is extremely painful and arduous to undertake the work of mourning. This was captured beautifully in Susie's description of her brother's capacity to move in and out of touch with the reality of his loss, as his desire to defend himself against pain waxed and waned. Heart to stone.

When mourning is not possible, recovery—the capacity to get on with life—is prevented. Instead, various pathological states, some based on identifications arising from the traumatic event, seem to offer a way for the person to keep going.

The process of recovery

How does one get on with life after a trauma? This is a common literary preoccupation. No wonder, because we all want to know what happens next—after the earthquake, after the murder, after the rape, after the terrorist attack.

The word recovery is misleading. It implies something regained, found again. After a traumatic event, life is never the same again. The desire to return to normal is a fantasy with a powerful seductive pull. All that can be recovered is life—whatever form that may take after a devastating event.

Consultations for trauma

The Unit for the Study of Trauma and Its Aftermath was conceived by Caroline Garland and a group of colleagues at the Tavistock Clinic soon after the *Herald of Free Enterprise* ferry disaster in 1986. It has developed through the clinical application of psychoanalytic theory to working with survivors of trauma, including those from subsequent public disasters including the King's Cross fire, the Hungerford massacre, the Hillsborough football stadium disaster, the Paddington train crash, September 11th, and the 2004 Asian tsunami. Many of the patients we see at the unit have faced events such as those of rape, assault, the murder of a loved one, and car accidents. The majority present months or even years after the trauma, long after the first stage of shock and helplessness has receded.

Building on experience, we have developed a model of working based on the notion of a brief, generally four-session, consultation. Sessions are 90 minutes long, usually spaced two to three weeks apart.

These arrangements may need to be modified. In recent years, we have seen increasing numbers of traumatized refugees from war-torn countries in Eastern Europe and Africa, as well as individuals tortured and traumatized by their own governments in the Middle East and South America. Their traumatic experiences have often been of a more chronic, repetitive, and sustained nature. A modified approach that we describe as intermittent treatment, taking place over a longer period, is often more appropriate in these circumstances.

We distinguish consultations from psychotherapy assessments. These patients are not referred for therapy. They have been sent to the unit for help, a need generated by an external traumatic event from which they have been unable to recover using the support available. The aim of our brief contact is to ascertain what has prevented recovery and, if possible, provide an opportunity for the patient to begin to mobilize his or her resources.

We are aware of the need to attend to practical matters such as housing, finances, immigration status, and so on, especially for asylum seekers and refugees. We also recognize the need to be flexible. If intrusive symptoms are prominent we may offer trauma-focused cognitive behavioural therapy. If it seems a mentalization-based approach would be helpful, we consider this. After a consultation, we may feel that group therapy would be appropriate for this particular patient. In the present context, however, I shall focus upon our psychoanalytically based therapeutic work. In order to frame what follows, I begin by considering what we mean by trauma.

The approach of descriptive psychiatry

Perhaps it would be helpful to characterize what is known as post-traumatic stress disorder (PTSD). PTSD occurs after a traumatic event that involved actual or threatened death or serious injury, or a threat to the physical integrity of self or others. Psychiatric criteria require the person to have experienced intense fear, helplessness, or horror when the event occurred. Traumatic events include physical, psychological, and sexual assault; terrorism and war; domestic violence; witnessing violence against others; and accidents and natural disasters. Approximately 50% of individuals will be exposed to at least one traumatic event in their lifetime. Approximately 8% of survivors will develop PTSD. Symptoms include re-experiencing and/or avoiding phenomena associated with the trauma, numbing, and increased arousal. They usually begin within three months of the incident but occasionally emerge years later. PTSD patients are six times more likely to attempt suicide than the general population.

It is worthwhile to distinguish PTSD from two other conditions. The first is "complex trauma" (Herman, 1992) resulting from chronic repetitive trauma. This may lead not only to symptoms of PTSD, but also clinical features of dissociation, somatization, re-victimization, affect dysregulation, and disruptions in identity. Herman emphasized that there was often a history of captivity or entrapment in the traumatic experience.

The second condition is developmental trauma disorder (van der Kolk, 2005), reflecting chronic or repetitive traumatization in childhood that has pervasive effects on the development of mind and brain. A child's capacity to integrate sensory, emotional, and cognitive information into a cohesive whole is affected.

If these descriptions summarize the untoward effects of trauma, how do we understand the sources and nature of those effects?

Psychoanalytic perspectives

In *Beyond the Pleasure Principle*, Freud (1920g) described trauma as a mental disturbance arising in people who survive devastating events that involve a risk to life. Here and in subsequent work, Freud stressed how a victim unprepared for danger and caught by surprise has an initial response of fright and an experience of helplessness (1926d [1925]). He also described attempts to deal with this by repeating the trauma in some form. In the new version of the trauma, one can initiate what happens, rather than having this come out of the blue; one might triumph over what happens, rather than being its victim. Freud observed that trauma appeared less likely to occur where there has been a physical injury. The injury seemed to bind "excesses of excitation" associated with the experience. In the absence of injury, a person can find it more difficult to assimilate what has happened.

Freud described trauma as piercing a protective shield around the mental apparatus. With this comes an emotional flooding, so that the usual discriminatory processes that protect the mind from being overwhelmed are lost. The traumatized person is faced with a barrage of internal anxieties and impulses alongside excessive stimulation from the traumatic event itself. Elaborating on the picture painted by Freud, Garland (1998) described trauma as the breaking down of established defences which are found to be inadequate to deal with the intensity of the event, the releasing of primitive horrors, and the consequent disruption and disintegration of the existing mental organization, with long-lasting consequences for the personality.

Garland describes two phases in the response to trauma. The first equates with Freud's description of a breach in the psychic shield. This is characterized by shock and a disintegration of mental functioning. It appears in the faces of survivors we see on our television screens, faces full of shock, horror, helplessness, and confusion. This phase can last for hours or days.

The second phase has two components. The traumatic experience stirs up powerful early anxieties. Often these include dread, horror, persecution, and falling apart. One may feel that all the goodness in the world is lost, along with an expectation of being protected and loved. As time goes on, the mind attempts to make sense of this experience in terms of what it already knows. Through a process that Freud called binding, the trauma becomes linked with disturbing events or difficult relationships rooted in the past.

Therefore, helplessness is central to trauma and its immediate aftermath. There is an urge, indeed urgency, to get rid of this experience.

Primitive meanings

Primitive anxieties are reawakened by trauma. The traumatic event is attributed to an agent, a someone or something who is responsible for what has happened to me. This results in an enormous sense of persecution by malevolent forces. Why would anyone do this to me? Alongside, there is a shattering of trust in goodness to protect one from harm, to prevent such things occurring. Meaning and reason have been lost.

Klein's (1946) description of the early infantile state of mind is helpful for understanding the anxieties faced by traumatized patients, as well as the defences they deploy. The trauma results in a reactivation of powerful, infantile anxieties from the paranoid-schizoid position of early infantile life (see chapter 10). As Segal (1957) has described, we have "pockets of vulnerability" within ourselves, sealed-off areas of primitive functioning representing developmental moments of trauma or inadequate containment that have not been worked through. These pockets are blown open by the trauma, so that the mind is flooded with powerful, primitive anxieties that may have been warded off for many years. The patient is overwhelmed by terror and dread, and anxieties of disintegration and death predominate. One's worst infantile fears are realized.

In the normal course of development, infants attempt to manage such unbearable anxieties by splitting their feelings and experiences into more manageable categories of very good and very bad. What is unbearable is split off and evacuated into the mind of another person by projective identification. Only slowly can a more integrated view of the world be achieved.

The traumatized mind attempts to find organization and meaning. Infantile experiences and relationships from the paranoid-schizoid position so powerfully reawakened by the trauma are bound to the event itself. The event comes to be understood at an unconscious level as a particular kind of relationship, one that confirms the most threatening aspects of early life. In this way, the event undergoes transformation into something recognizable, according to the template of an early relationship that evoked anxiety and dread. At least this is familiar—I have been here before.

Through close observation of the transference and countertrans-ference during a consultation, a therapist can become aware of the unconscious links that have been made in this way. Past relation-ships have given the current trauma unconscious meanings, and there is a powerful need to replicate aspects of those relationships in the transference as part of the repetition compulsion. The need for action and re-enactment is especially strong because the person's symbolic capacities have been compromised. Victims of trauma are less able to use verbal memory and their own life-narratives to understand what has happened, and to think about its meaning. Instead, action in various forms is all that is available.

Words

This brings us to the importance of words. Trauma disrupts the capacity to use symbols. One loses the imaginative space in which to think. When reality collides with our omnipotent wishes and primitive anxieties, there is a collapse in the space between imagination and external reality. One no longer has faith in being able to imagine something as being different from it actually happening. In this way, the thought becomes the agent of the event, and the memory is the event itself. This begins to explain why survivors re-experience traumatic events and suffer flashbacks. With the loss of symbolic functioning, certain words can assume a role stripped of their value and meaning. They become symbolic equations—that is, they become equated with what they are supposed to represent. In a newspaper article, a survivor of the 2005 London bombings reported that there were some words that she was unable to say because she felt them as something literally ripping into her flesh, just as the original trauma had done.

Loss and mourning

All trauma involves loss of one kind or another. Some of these losses are easier to see and understand than others: the loss of one's pre-trauma physical state, the loss of friends or loved ones, the loss of a certain way of life; loss of hope, loss of identity, loss of feeling. Less obvious losses include that of relinquishing a particular view of the world, once one faces mortality. If one has to acknowledge one's own potential for aggression and face the extent of human destructiveness, one may lose a vision of oneself and mankind.

Freud's classic paper "Mourning and Melancholia" (1917e [1915]) serves as a foundation for understanding loss and its consequences. The work of mourning after losing a loved person involves an acceptance of the reality of the loss and withdrawal of all attachments to that person. The slow and painful nature of this work requires each memory and expectation to be examined and the reality acknowledged. Freud saw the work of mourning as detaching investment (libido) from the person (object). A complementary view is that in mourning, one needs to reclaim those parts of oneself that have been projected into someone else through projective identification. In other words, one needs to own what one has located in the other person. Therefore, acknowledging the reality of loss can be intimately related to achieving differentiation between self and other. Each of these may be important for mourning to proceed.

There are a number of factors that may make the work of mourning too difficult and thereby may hinder or prevent recovery. Among the factors to consider are a person's very early experiences with primary caregivers, especially experiences of containment or otherwise; the stage of psychic development (both past and present) during which trauma has taken place; the nature of the traumatic event; guilt; and the degree of the person's ambivalence and hostility.

To recover from loss requires working through the process of mourning. Without mourning, a precarious contact with reality ensues. Instead, there exists a kind of private reality where time stands still, where past becomes present and present past, a psychic retreat from the overwhelming pain, guilt, fury, and sadness that mourning threatens.

Where guilt is present, reparation in either symbolic or actual terms is necessary. For the traumatized patient, this is made more difficult by the degree of guilt that may occur. The severity of the trauma may be such that a person feels unable to make amends. The person may feel he or she has insufficient internal or external capacities to set things right. Moreover, as Freud (1915b) describes in "Thoughts for the Times on War and Death", the loss of a loved one provokes a particular form of guilt that he called survivor guilt. This is based on the notion that all loved relationships contain ambivalent feelings of love and hate. Even the smallest degree of hate leads to triumph, if only unconsciously, at the death of the other, as this is experienced as though it were the death of the rival or enemy. When one has survived an event in which others have died, guilt is going to feature prominently.

A person may seek to avoid guilt by identifying with dead or damaged people and internal objects, as Freud described. If one gives up anything pleasurable or lively and forsakes life, one may avoid the psychic pain of mourning. Alternatively, one might turn away from one's own aggression and hostility by assuming a persistent victim state, whereby aggression is both attributed to and stirred up in others. If it becomes impossible to take back these parts of oneself, then mourning is not possible and a person is left more vulnerable to external re-enactments that perpetuate the victim state.

There is another impediment to resolving the challenges of traumatic experience. When it feels that something painful and unpleasant has been done to oneself, there is a natural pull towards an identification with the person felt to be the cause. If one identifies with the aggressor, then one becomes an agent rather than a helpless victim, and the door for revenge is open.

On top of all this, as we have seen, traumatized patients have a limited capacity for symbolization, if only in the area of the trauma itself. This makes it difficult for the person to find the words to describe what he or she feels, to understand what has happened, and to incorporate this into his or her own narrative. I believe that Alice Sebold's efforts to find words to describe her experiences contributed to the healing and reparative qualities of her creative novel.

Treatment

Caroline Garland (2005) writes:

> Treatment begins with the sense of being listened to by someone whose intention is to understand. If the therapist can take in something of the magnitude of what has happened to the patient, internally and externally, without being totally overwhelmed by it, there is a hope once more of re-establishing a world with meaning in it. [p. 249]

The importance of containment of this kind cannot be overestimated. In consultations, a therapist is required to take in overwhelming experiences without becoming overwhelmed him/herself. Profound anxieties and hostility are part of what the trauma patient is unable to bear. The therapist needs to register and contain such feelings sufficiently if the patient is going to come to contain and integrate such feelings him/herself.

This demonstrates why the therapeutic relationship, rather than the event itself, is central for the consultation. The relationship that develops between patient and therapist has features that reflect early experiences which have been taken to provide meaning for the traumatic event. Through containing and addressing what emerges in the therapeutic relationship, a psychotherapist may ameliorate the untoward consequences of both past and present events. It may seem paradoxical, but working in the transference allows the patient a deeper and more thorough exploration and understanding of the meaning of the traumatic event. Discovering such meaning, with its unconscious as well as conscious dimensions, allows a patient to make sense of his or her own distressing responses to trauma.

Case vignette: Mr A

One winter's night, two young men, somewhat intoxicated from recent celebrations, hop on to a beaten-up old motorbike and begin the drive home. They come from the same market town and have known each other most of their lives. At a slippery corner, the driver loses control, hurling them straight into the path of an oncoming lorry.

The driver died, and his friend, Mr A, sustained serious injury and spent a considerable time in hospital. Mr A was in his early twenties. He was successful in business, in a somewhat reckless manner. He had spent much of his youth actively seeking out a variety of death-defying activities, including bungee-jumping, parachuting, and motorcycle racing.

After initial shock, anger, and disbelief, Mr A managed the months of hospitalization and physical recovery by becoming the model patient. The nurses spoke of what an impressive young man he was, always doing what he should, and obliging the staff in any way he could. As Mr A began to find his way back into the world and start to pick up the pieces of his life, incredulity, shock, and a sense of chaos began to recede.

Then three months after discharge from hospital, Mr A came to feel increasingly depressed, hopeless, and despairing. He began to have nightmares. These were vivid, powerful reconstructions of the accident, which left him screaming and shivering in their aftermath. He found himself increasingly unable to fall asleep, to get into a car, or to be around people. He was tense, often angry, and easily startled. Thoughts seemed to turn again and again to his lost friend. Mr A felt that if only he had stopped him from driving that night, none of this would have happened. He found himself unable to return to his life, unable to communicate his distress to friends or family, increasingly guilt-ridden and with thoughts of suicide.

When Mr A came to see me, I was immediately struck by what a likeable, helpful, and obliging chap he was. However, in telling his story to me, suddenly Mr A would say something that had a shocking and almost jaw-dropping effect. For instance, he was speaking in a rather general way about the injuries he had sustained. Then suddenly he switched into giving me a minutely detailed, grisly, and gory account of exactly what his leg had looked like at the scene of the accident. The effect on me was to feel shocked, horrified, and taken aback. Something like this happened on a number of occasions. When he delivered these blows, momentarily I was left reeling. Mr A, in contrast, seemed almost bright and breezy.

As Mr A's history gradually unfolded, he gave a vivid account of a violent, unpredictable father and a rather masochistic, self-effacing mother. Mr A remembered that as a child he would be sleeping peacefully in his bed when his father would come to him and slap him repeatedly across the face. No explanation was given, and Mr A's mother never intervened. His response was to try to be as well behaved as possible, keeping himself hidden from his father's eyes by becoming like his self-effacing mother.

My sense was that Mr A's experience of these parents, with

father's unpredictable violence and mother's masochism, provided a template for his interpretation of the accident. The event was experienced by Mr A as a kind of unexpected, violent slap in the face. His response was to behave as he had before and become the good little boy, doing everything he was meant to in order to prevent further punishment. Yet he was left with a serious disability, a slap from which his defences offered no protection.

One may surmise that even prior to his trauma, Mr A was attempting to master the anxieties of his childhood experiences (while also risking another slap in the face) by death-defying activities such as parachuting and bungee-jumping. There is a fusion of life and death instincts in the compulsion to repeat, because repetition also promises the possibility of a different outcome. But now Mr A's accident had ripped open pockets of vulnerability, and unprocessed primitive anxieties became linked with the current trauma.

Loss of symbolic functioning added to Mr A's inclination towards action and further repetition of trauma. The trauma could be neither symbolized nor mourned, and so it was repeated. Not only this, but in the consultation, Mr A would identify with the aggressor and project barely manageable feeling as he repeatedly slapped me in the face. Containment and understanding of such interpersonal enactments seemed to offer the best chance that the impasse might be resolved and Mr A's development and integration proceed.

I turn now to describe someone with complex trauma. This person presented with somatization, re-victimization, affect dysregulation, and disruptions in identity, along with symptoms of PTSD.

Case vignette: Ms B

Ms B's body kept the score of a prolonged experience of incarceration, torture, and rape. This had occurred when she was living in her war-torn homeland as a married woman with three children. She had been suspected of subversive activity by the government and was arrested and imprisoned.

During her incarceration, Ms B was repeatedly tortured and raped. In between these events she was left in a cell with one other woman who, after several days, died from her injuries. Ms B was sure that she would also be killed. At one point, the right side of her head was shaven and she was humiliated and beaten in front of several guards. It was unclear why she was allowed to leave, but after several weeks she was released. Her husband was missing, presumed dead. Ms B managed to escape across the border with her children and, against considerable adversity, found a new life for herself.

Now Ms B was plagued by headaches on the right side of her head, as well as chest pains that were deemed to be non-organic. She had chronically poorly controlled diabetes. She had symptoms of depression alongside classical features of PTSD, especially intrusive phenomena and hypervigilance.

Ms B was referred by her GP after she had been compulsorily detained for several weeks in a psychiatric unit. The admission seemed to have arisen out of increasing concern about her mental state. She had also expressed suicidal thoughts.

In the room with Ms B, rapidly I began to feel tired as I strained to listen to her high-pitched whisper. Any movement or noise would cause her to jump and scan the room for threat. I found myself experiencing headaches after our meetings, accompanied by a sense of needing to do something quickly. It became clear how Ms B had injected so much anxiety into the system for this to lead to her psychiatric detention. In a concrete manner, Ms B had experienced the compulsory admission as a repetition of her previous incarceration. Now there was an enormous pressure for me to become the good object who was going to protect her from these experiences occurring again.

Ms B would sit with me, holding her head, whispering her complaints against the psychiatric team, jumping if I moved or began to say anything. I found myself immobilized, helpless in the face of her distress. When she recounted the story of the other woman in her cell, it became possible to see how much her own experience of helplessness was being enacted.

As we began to consider this together, it became possible to think about Ms B's fury, and how much of this was being directed against her body. It was as though her body had become both the prison that held her and the torturer. Ms B was using her body to act out a masochistic state of mind that used suffering as a means to avoid persecutory guilt. The physical symptoms represented a kind of refuge from something dangerous and persecutory within herself. Ms B's headaches seemed to be a concrete expression, held in her body, of the traumatic experience and what it stirred.

At different times, Ms B enacted different aspects of the trauma. Her identification with the aggressor was reflected in the transference in my feeling helpless and pinned down by her anxiety, as well as with Ms B's treatment of her own body. She identified with the dead or damaged other in her melancholia, thereby evading guilt. Her somatic symptoms, too, were a way of not-remembering, as unbearable feelings were disavowed and discharged instead through the body. Ms B re-enacted the victim state in her interaction with the psychiatric team. She repeated her incarceration through the hospitalization. If the psychiatric team were perpetrators, I was to be the rescuer. Indeed, Ms B herself could be victim, perpetrator, witness, or rescuer.

Of course, all that I have described needs to be set in broader context. Refugees such as Ms B may have faced multiple bereavements including loss of country, status, activity, cultural reference points, social networks, and family. They may have faced persistent and intensive persecution, witnessed violence inflicted on loved ones, or had violence senselessly committed against them. At times, this may have been part of systematized and brutal torture and degradation. At some point they have had to flee, to pull up roots and escape to an unknown fate awaiting them in a strange and often hostile land. Realities such as these need to be acknowledged, never neglected.

Final thoughts

I end this chapter by highlighting a few technical points about brief psychoanalytic work with traumatized patients. I do so in a series of short paragraphs.

The traumatic event is not the focus of treatment. The therapeutic task is to understand the meaning of the event and what may interfere with mourning. This requires attention to the nature of a person's internal world. A primary aim is to trace how past and present have become entwined, following the trauma.

Following trauma, one essential task is that of mourning.

Trauma reactivates primitive anxieties and impairs symbolic functioning. Therefore, patients are more likely to have a persecutory response to the analytic setting. The therapist needs to be aware of this, particularly in relation to silences or "blank-screen" models of working.

There is always a push for action, played out in the transference. Often this includes a person identifying with elements from the original traumatic scenario. Work in the transference and countertransference allows for an understanding of the unconscious meaning of the traumatic event.

The therapist may be required to bear what is unbearable for the patient, as part of the therapeutic process of containment. Aggression and destructiveness need to be faced and owned. A therapist might need to allow him/herself to be an idealized or denigrated object, before it is possible for the patient to be aware of his or her own aggression.

At the same time, a therapist needs to respect the defences the patient has employed to continue to function in a world that has been decimated by trauma. If the patient comes to face a choice over whether to bear the pain of mourning traumatic losses, then that choice is the patient's.

For many complex trauma patients, especially asylum seekers and refugees, psychotherapy may need to be modified to allow full acknowledgement and management of external reality.

In summary, psychoanalytic psychotherapy offers the opportunity to understand what has happened and continues to happen (both internally and externally) in response to trauma.

Trauma disrupts, disturbs, and dislocates time, language, and truth. Working with traumatized patients requires potency, authenticity, and respect. Difficult countertransference experiences are inevitable, and containment, supervision, and support of the therapeutic work is vital.

CHAPTER 9

Very troubled patients

David Bell & Birgit Kleeberg

T here is a tendency to think that psychotherapy services are for less disturbed patients, but psychotherapists who have worked in the NHS know just how foreign this is to their clinical experience. A large proportion of the patients referred for psychotherapy suffer from lifelong difficulties covering a wide variety of diagnoses, including "borderline", "schizoid", "bipolar", "severe depression", and "eating disorders", and, of course, these categories are not mutually exclusive. Many patients are or have been at serious risk of self-harm or suicide, and some have suffered from manifest psychosis.

These are people who have profound problems in managing human relationships, and so, naturally, they bring these problems to the relationship with professionals who are charged with their care. Sometimes they are referred for this very reason—that is, because they have stirred up unmanageable (often unacknowledged) feelings in health care professionals. They are often regarded as "difficult" as well as very troubled.

The above list spans the categories of "illness" and "personality disorder". This is not surprising, for from a psychoanalytic perspective the discontinuity in personhood implied by this contrast is more apparent than real. When examined in detail, the outbreak of manifest illness tends to express, sometimes in bizarre and distorted form, conflicts and preoccupations that were part of the personality prior to the breakdown. Thus what *appears* as illness is understood, psychoanalytically, as a *personality development*, under the stress of certain internal and external conditions.

Individuals who become ill suffer from a kind of "fault line" in the structure of their personality. Under the pressure of a toxic interaction between a sensitized internal world and malign external circumstances, this reaches the point of breakdown. Where more benign circumstances prevail, the fault line continues as a source of continuous anxiety, but illness may not become manifest. So, too, in the case of psychiatric disorder involving multiple "comorbid" conditions, the different parts of a complex picture are likely to reflect different facets of the individual's character and personality.

This chapter focuses on patients with these more difficult and complex problems, and we shall be drawing on our clinical experience in the specialist service of the Fitzjohn's Unit of the Tavistock Clinic. In a manner reminiscent of Freud's description of neurotic people who reveal what the rest of us keep secret, these more disturbed patients can bring to our attention far-reaching psychodynamic issues that may otherwise remain hidden.

The assessment process

The term "assessment" reinforces the idea that a patient is being subjected to an examination that he or she might pass or fail. This is likely to be especially unhelpful for very troubled patients, for whom the dice are already heavily loaded towards this disturbing binary view.

Mr C was referred to our service having had various treatments. Nothing had seemed to help. He arrived, entered the room, and waited a few minutes. He then said: "I want to have psychotherapy, and so it seems to me that I need to know what I must do in this meeting to ensure I get the treatment that, from what I understand, is likely to be most helpful."

Mr C makes this issue explicit, but it is likely that similar influences operate with less disturbed patients, albeit in a more hidden, subtle way. There is much to be said for referring to the meeting not as an assessment but as a consultation, with the implication that a number of outcomes are possible.

Mr C reminds us of something else—namely, that patients arrive full of conscious and unconscious preconceptions and beliefs not only about the consultation, but also about the kind of treatment being offered. Such expectations will have been set in motion by a combination of the patient's own inner preoccupations *and* the reinforcement these have or have not received from the referral process itself.

Case vignette: Ms D

Ms D had suffered very serious deprivation in childhood. She had been known to the local psychiatric services for many years and had attracted a plethora of diagnoses and treatments. She had been admitted on a number of occasions, and always it was difficult to discharge her. The referring team felt exhausted. They conveyed to the patient how they were seeking specialist, intensive treatment for her. But Ms D's understanding of "specialist" and "intensive" was very different from what the team had intended to communicate. These words stirred up very primitive longings, so Ms D felt that at last she was going to be offered a longed-for situation where all needs would be gratified. "Intensive" treatment unconsciously meant to her that someone would be completely available, so she would no longer face the feelings of separation and abandonment that had dominated much of her life.

And so the scene was set for a disturbing encounter. For Ms D, the meeting was a kind of Kafkaesque rite of passage. She experienced the psychotherapist as an archaic father/guard on an entry door to an idealized maternal figure, and so it was inevitable that she would be disappointed.

Of course, there are many ways in which such encounters can be played out. For example, a patient may sabotage the consultation in order to ensure he or she does not get help, thereby assuaging a masochistic need for punishment. Our point is that the consultation process, especially with more troubled patients, can be overwhelmed by the effects of these primitive mental processes. In those cases where this occurs most powerfully, it is most difficult to see and to hold on to a balanced perspective.

Even experienced clinicians can succumb to this difficulty, and psychotherapists may go to great lengths to justify themselves to the patient. They may end up offering a treatment that they do not really think is likely to be helpful, either as an act of submission or in an attempt to fend off complaints. Yet in the face of great pressure, it is critical to maintain balance, and this is, perhaps, one of the most important determinants of whether the outcome of a consultation is or is not therapeutic.

It is not enough for a psychotherapist to focus attention on characteristics that belong to the ("suitable" or "unsuitable") patient, for there are many interacting factors to consider when thinking about the possibility of psychotherapy. As Murray Jackson was prone to ask: "What particular patient, with what kind of difficulties, living in what kind of social context with what kind of psychotherapist, with what kind of supervision, with what kind of back up (e.g. from local psychiatric services), and within what social context?" It may make sense for a patient with a particular kind of difficulty to embark on psychotherapy in one context, whereas it would not be appropriate in another.

Case vignette: Mr E

Mr E was a very severely disturbed man who had made a number of suicide attempts. In reviewing the course of his treatment, one could see that there was a pattern of negative therapeutic reactions—that is, the possibility of progress led to a worsening of symptoms. Just at the point where he seemed to be improving, Mr E would suddenly deteriorate and make another suicide attempt, perhaps prompted by feelings of guilt or hatred of feeling needy and dependent. Yet despite the profound despair and frustration he induced in those around him, the psychiatric team had not allowed themselves to become alienated from Mr E. They had a fairly realistic view of the dangers of embarking on psychotherapy, and they had made it clear that they would continue to see Mr E regularly, maintain contact with his key worker, and share responsibility in all decision-making. They also understood that psychotherapy might not help, and, even if it did, there was bound to be an escalation of acting out.

A major factor that led to our offering Mr E psychotherapy was the support on which he and we could draw as he embarked on this inevitably disturbing venture.

By contrast, another patient, Ms F, revealed during the consultation that she spent all day sitting alone in her room and had practically no social contact. Although Ms F showed herself to be, at least to some extent, interested in understanding herself, it did not seem appropriate for her to embark on psychotherapy.

When patients with such a meagre social life commence psychotherapy, they can come to feel it is the only thing they have in their lives. They will spend much of their time ruminating over the contents of the last session, and awaiting the next. Here it is may be better to engage the help of a Community Mental Health Team (CMHT) in an attempt to mobilize the patient's investment in the world. If this is successful, psychotherapy may become a more realistic prospect.

On occasion, in such situations we have even made a kind of contract with a patient, suggesting that if the person can enrol in a course or take on a voluntary job, then we will seriously reconsider the possibility of psychotherapy. We would contrast this stance with another that may seem similar, but is different. We do *not* find it helpful to establish a treatment contract with patients of the kind, "If you don't cut more, then you can stay in treatment", because this may provoke perverse entanglement. When it comes to psychotherapy itself, we would merely anticipate that if things do rapidly deteriorate in the course of psychotherapy, then we could decide at the time whether to plan a meeting to end the treatment earlier than intended.

It has to be acknowledged that assessment is a blunt tool, and so we should not overvalue its predictive capacity. No matter how careful we are, we make mistakes. There are patients who were thought to be unsuitable but who, had they been given the chance, may well have proved their assessor wrong. At times, we accept patients who reveal themselves to be unable to use psychotherapy or who make use of it in a malignantly destructive manner. Some individuals who in the consultation process seem to score highly on some imaginary scale of ego function, or of the capacity to use understanding, present a completely different picture once they embark on therapy. Britton has described the way an analyst may, in the context of a consultation, be able to talk to the patient *about* "it"—namely, some very disturbed part of the patient's character. But once analysis gets under way, the patient no longer talks about, but becomes, "it".

Many patients who are referred have been disturbed for a very long time, perhaps for most of their lives. So a question presents itself: "Why now?" In many cases it is a breakdown that brings patients to treatment—that is, their familiar defences have failed them, and they become overwhelmed with feelings of acute anxiety and despair. The structure that has provided them with a precarious stability up until this point constitutes their own unique combination of anxieties and defences; in other words, their character structure. To some extent, this has protected them from psychic pain, and now their most pressing concern is to be free of pain (which is, of course, entirely reasonable). So it is to be expected that they will endeavour to re-establish their previous defensive structure, and this may become apparent even in the consultation.

One familiar scenario is where a patient has been looked after by a CMHT, but the clinician who has been most responsible for his or her care is leaving. This generates considerable anxiety in relation to the consequences of the pending separation. Not infrequently, this goes unmentioned, and instead the referral may be framed in terms of the patient "coming to a point of wanting to consider psychotherapy". Then, at the end of the letter, the referrer writes: "As I have come to the end of my post here, please reply to Dr X who will be taking over from me next month." In other situations, a team may be failing to contain a patient; here, one option is to arrange a consultation to address *the team's* fault lines, as these have been revealed by the patient.

Another familiar kind of referral is that of patients who had been (say) cutting themselves very badly but had stopped for a period of time, perhaps when taking on a new job. Understandably, a clinical management team may have the idea that, now things are stable, the patient might be considered for psychotherapy in order to get to grips with the underlying problem. Only sometimes is this idea well founded. Not infrequently, it is better to support and acknowledge what the local service has achieved and *not* go along with the idea that formal psychotherapy can do better. The potential disruption of stability is also apparent in those patients who do very well while on the waiting list, but become acutely disturbed when a vacancy arises and treatment starts. It is as if they are most comfortable in a world where treatment will be offered—but only in the future, never now.

Whatever the background to a referral, it is vital that, in the consultation, the clinician makes space for the more disturbed parts of the patient to come into the room. There are real dangers of conveying to a patient, however unwittingly, that more severe levels of disturbance will not be tolerated. When this happens, patient and therapist are drawn into a tacit agreement that the more disturbed elements will be kept out of view. This creates a kind of pseudo-alliance, which, when the degree of splitting can no longer be maintained, breaks down.

Nevertheless, one needs to do one's best to judge whether psychotherapy is likely to be helpful. When conducting consultations, we are not looking for the patient to prove him/herself. Our default position is to assume that the patient can be helped, unless we are led to think otherwise. In this regard, one of the most important issues to address is the patient's availability to understanding.

Case vignette: Mrs G

Mrs G came into the consultation room, sat down, and patiently waited for me [one of the authors] to say something. It was clear she expected a battery of questions. I invited her to tell me something about herself. She spent some time listing her symptoms along with details of their duration, evolution, and intransigence. An atmosphere of deadening despair entered the room as she talked about herself in this alienated and objectified manner. After a while, I said to her: "It is as if you are describing an ill self which you wish to hand over for me to examine. Then I shall let you know what kind of treatment I wish to prescribe, without you participating at all."

This led to a palpable shift in the atmosphere. Mrs G began to weep, and she said: "I do not think I have really ever properly participated in anything in my life." Paradoxically, it was clear that at this moment she was more alive and participating, but in a manner that was, for her, very disturbing. As the meeting went on, not surprisingly Mrs G reached again for deadening defences to protect herself from this painful turmoil, yet one could see that the situation was fluid so that it made sense for her to embark on psychotherapy. In this case, a deepening of understanding was accompanied by a broadening of the contact with the patient, and the therapist had a sense of something mobile both in the patient–therapist interaction and within Mrs G's own mind.

Only sometimes does this kind of deeper contact bring evolution within the consultation. At other times it is fleeting, but even here it has great importance, as it points to the possibility of forming a therapeutic alliance. When deeply entrenched defences show little sign of movement, it can be vital to carry out further consultations to provide an adequate opportunity for this kind of development to occur.

It is through an engagement that foregrounds the way the patient is *relating* that a psychotherapist is able to apprehend the person's psychopathology as a dynamic structure. This and only this can provide the basis for an adequate assessment of what the patient is both seeking and able to tolerate.

The dimension of perversity

It might be thought that someone's availability to understanding co-varies with severity of psychopathology in a linear way. One might suppose that the more severely ill a patient, the less that person's capacity for being interested in him/herself. This turns out not to be the case. There are many patients referred for psychotherapy who would have low scores on any ordinary scale of disturbance but who, in the context of a psychoanalytic consultation, reveal themselves to be very heavily defended against or even aversive to any possibility of self-knowledge. In such circumstances, the patient should be allowed a dignified retreat. On the other hand, it is not unusual to find very disturbed patients, including some who would be classed as psychotic, who respond well to attempts to understand them and then go on to make good use of psychotherapy.

One of the distinctions that we have found to be of great practical value is that between those states where a significant degree of perversity dominates the clinical picture and those where this is not the case. By the term "perversity", we refer to situations where the patient derives pleasure, often quite secret pleasure, from his or her deterioration and from frustrating the therapist's attempts to help. This pattern may have both masochistic and sadistic qualities. Masochistic pleasure may be derived from the patient's own self-destruction and sadistic pleasure from the tormented relationships formed with others.

This "dimension of perversity" is relatively independent of psychiatric diagnosis and is a serious problem that often goes unrecognized, especially when there is a focus on diagnosis rather than patients' ways of relating to themselves and the world around them. Whereas psychiatric consultation produces something like a still photograph, a psychoanalytic perspective unfolds more like a film that reveals psychopathology—sometimes including perversity—as a *living* phenomenon in the relationship between the patient and his or her world.

Consider two hypothetical patients, each of whom has strong suicidal feelings and impulses. In the less perverse patient, the wish to live is, as it were, "handed over" (projected into) the staff caring for him or her. But the motive here is to protect more hopeful and life-sustaining attitudes from powerful destructive forces within the patient. The patient does not yet have a self strong enough to withstand a primitive part of the personality (superego), which takes an inwardly punitive stance, and he or she is relieved that others take on some responsibility for his or her survival. Then, with the capacity to form a working alliance with a therapist, the patient can gain in strength and gradually take back the wish to live.

In the more perverse situation, the aim is different. The more the patient rids him/herself of the wish to live, the more he or she idealizes death. Often this is accompanied by feelings of triumph. A patient such as this can become contemptuous of those who are trying to help and can even sneer at efforts to keep him or her alive. Having said this, when perverse modes of functioning are predominantly defensive, they may be available for analysis and even relinquished in the course of psychotherapy.

The question of abuse

Sometimes patients are referred for their having suffered sexual abuse, as if this alone constitutes justification for the referral. Once again, the patients' ways of relating to themselves and others are what really matter. And, of course, such ways of relating can have a powerful influence on other people's behaviour and experience.

Mr H, a man in his twenties, had been sexually abused and severely neglected as a child. The referral from his GP included a newspaper cutting describing a recent court case with details of the horrible abuse this man had suffered as a child. One had the impression that the publicity surrounding the case was linked to the reason for referral. It seemed that the GP did not want to be seen to be negligent. But enclosing the cutting was perhaps also a way of concretely handing on undigested awareness of this terrible situation.

In the event, the patient did not attend any of the appointments offered. This was despite the fact that he kept in touch and ensured that he was sent further appointments. He became angry when, in a letter, it was suggested that his non-attendance may indicate ambivalence about pursuing psychotherapy and that he might want to discuss this with his GP. It seemed to us that the patient needed to maintain contact with the possibility of getting help but dreaded it ever happening. Such patients often believe they will, in the consultation, "have to talk about the abuse", which would be likely to stir up unmanageable feelings.

Some patients and referrers have the idea that describing the abuse, perhaps in detail over and over again, is helpful; however, it needs to be recognized that some patients have to wall-off feelings in order to get on with their lives. This may not be pathological, and defences may need respecting. If the walls are demolished—for example, when sexually abused patients testify against their abusers in court—this can lead to breakdown and an enduring deterioration in functioning. We have had patients who have felt under pressure from their local service to come into psychotherapy in order to talk about the abuse they suffered as a child, but who in a consultation are relieved by being freed of this pressure and having their need to protect themselves acknowledged and accepted.

On not offering psychotherapy
Case vignette: Ms I

Ms I, a 40-year-old childless Brazilian woman with a history of depression and a suicide attempt, was referred by a consultant psychiatrist. She had disclosed to the psychiatrist that in her childhood there had been extensive sexual and physical abuse perpetrated by her mother and stepfather. She felt responsible and deserving of this abuse. As a means of managing intense feelings, memories, and flashbacks, she had been self-cutting since early adolescence. Previously Ms I had received different forms of psychotherapy. She remained under the care of the CMHT, and she occasionally made use of their crisis and out-of-hours service.

In the questionnaire that we send all patients, Ms I wrote that she has so many "issues" that she loses orientation and does not know what to address. In describing her childhood, she made no reference to either of her parents. She wrote about feeling completely alone with her worries. There was an aunt to whom she would turn when upset as a child. She had done well at school and university and was now working as a science teacher. She had felt very bad after having had an operation on the scars caused by her self-harm, and she wrote that maybe that had triggered the suicide attempt.

Waiting by the lift prior to the first consultation, the clinician noticed an angelic-looking woman emerging from an unexpected direction. She seemed to be looking for something and walked right past her. When the therapist caught up with her and led her into the consulting room, she left the door wide open and looked completely lost. She said she did not know what the meeting was for, and that she had been sent here. She didn't know what kind of place this was.

The psychotherapist addressed Ms I's sense of disorientation, and Ms I said it would feel easier if she was asked questions. The therapist pointed out that that would create a situation where she was responding to what someone else wanted. This seemed to be what she felt in relation to being here—that she was sent, and that someone else thought this might be a good idea. Ms I agreed and said that it was not something that she would have thought of. Later in the meeting, she described how it was her partner who had persuaded her to have surgery to remove her scars.

Ms I conveyed she felt hopeless that anything could change. She said she had learnt not to expect anything, because she could not bear to be disappointed. She had anticipated that maybe having a job would make things different, but things had not worked out that way. She spoke of feeling bad about almost everything she did.

The therapist asked: "Almost everything?" Ms I replied: "One thing I think I can do is teach science, but I'm not saying that I am good with young people. None of my colleagues would say that I am bad with them, but no one knows how difficult it is for me." She continued: "When I had psychotherapy there was somewhere to put these things, and also to leave these things. But my partner thought things were worse when I was having psychotherapy." She said nothing about her childhood, and the therapist felt it was not a topic that could be addressed in the consultation.

The therapist had a chilling association in response to meeting Ms I. This was to a scene in the film *The Downfall*, about the last days of Hitler and his entourage in the bunker in Berlin, where Goebbels' wife is poisoning her children. This led the therapist to see the patient as both victim and perpetrator in a deadly scene of this kind. In her inner world, the patient seemed subject to a relationship with a figure who could not tolerate any imperfection or blemish, and to be wedded to the idea that such blemishes have to be eradicated. Overall, it felt to the therapist that Ms I was like a dazed child who would follow one blindly, as if enthralled by a deeply flawed parental figure.

The CMHT provided support and management, and they reported no problem with Ms I's work as a teacher. We were struck by how dismissive Ms I was towards her own capacities, and we became concerned that the well-functioning network that was containing and supporting Ms I had also lost its sense of doing a good job. The degree of perversity evident from the history and the manner in which Ms I presented to the assessor led us to believe that it was too dangerous to offer her psychotherapy— we considered that to do so would be to collude with the omnipotent idea that all damage and scars can be removed. We thought psychotherapy would be more likely to exacerbate Ms I's destructiveness and might well lead to suicidal feelings. In our judgment, Ms I was receiving optimal help already, although (as in some other cases of early developmental trauma linked to sexual abuse) we did give serious thought to referring her on for inpatient psychotherapy.

On risking psychotherapy
Case vignette: Ms J

Here we describe what happened when someone who, despite presenting with high risk and some perverse tendencies, was accepted for psychotherapy. We follow this case beyond the initial consultation to illustrate how the outcome may be finely balanced between benefit and potential harm.

Ms J was a middle-aged woman referred by a consultant psychiatrist after she (the patient) had become frustrated with non-psychoanalytic psychotherapy. She was a perfectionist, but she cut herself secretly.

The initial part of the consultation interview was very difficult. The therapist became increasingly aware of Ms J's need for control, as well as a great deal of self-contempt. Ms J used the phrase: " if I am to gain admission". She felt she was going to be admitted into something that would provide for her and relieve her from the burden of the constant persecution that she had suffered all her life. The therapist also noted how Ms J used the word "audition" to describe the process they were engaged in. It turned out that Ms J saw many things she did in life as performing, rather than being herself.

There was battle for control at the commencement of the interview, but in due course this began to ease. However, the therapist was very concerned about the patient's cutting and put it to Ms J that they were dealing with quite serious and destructive feelings, which might be stirred up by embarking on treatment.

Ms J seemed to understand this. At the same time, she was capable of twisting the therapist's meaning, as if he had insisted that she had to cure herself in order to receive treatment. Yet in the end, in part because of the supports available for treatment, Ms J was offered psychotherapy.

Within weeks of the start of Ms J's twice-weekly psychotherapy, the self-harm began to escalate. Following a session in which there was some real emotional contact with her psychotherapist, Ms J cut alarmingly close to a major artery. She conveyed a perverse dimension to her behaviour, describing scenes of locking herself in the bathroom for long periods of time as her mother knocked anxiously on the door, and taking pleasure in her mother's escalating fear and frustration. This captured the situation experienced by the therapist, who was made aware of the possibility of something terrifyingly destructive going on but was shut out, with no access to any concern in the patient. Ms J could not bear to feel small, helpless, or distressed, such feelings being diminished by her active self-harming.

Despite all these difficulties, over the first year Ms J appeared to derive some benefit from psychotherapy and at times showed a real capacity for concern, and the serious self-harm diminished. She became involved in a very disturbed affair in which both partners seemed to be torturing each other. She would feel alternately very needy in relation to her partner (associated with feeling suicidal) or rejecting and abusive (associated with cutting herself).

After the first Christmas break, which was difficult for her to manage, Ms J returned to say she had had a successful holiday, had ended the affair, and had begun to think of starting a family with a man she had long known. She could easily not have survived the last year, she felt. She spoke of what she had, in particular her job and her resumed old relationship, each of which she could so easily have lost. She said that her first priority should be to maintain both, and she went on to say that she had decided to end the therapy.

We thought Ms J had regained some equilibrium during the break and was terrified that this would be disturbed by returning to the sessions. It became clear that she felt there was an area inside her that was full of terrifying feelings. Yet she also felt she had some control, in the sense of being able to lock them away. To receive help was to cause trouble internally, and Ms J knew it could easily lead to dangerous enactments. It was clearly important that the therapist was not critical of Ms J's decision to end the therapy, that this was not viewed as a failure, and that future re-referral was possible. Ms J left in a thoughtful way.

Conclusion

In offering consultations to very troubled patients, it is very important to be flexible, as patients are individuals who cannot be fitted into a formula nor slotted into an agenda. Given that many have such harsh figures in their internal worlds, we need to be careful neither to submit to nor avoid these, but at the same time not become confused with the figures and so add to the patient's torments.

Our aims are modest. We do not expect patients to emerge from therapy in a radically altered state. Indeed, it is often a major achievement for therapist as well as patient to throw off the tyrannical idea that the person *should* recover. Even individuals who are unable to change very much can find the experience of being understood both profound and immensely valuable. When patients feel their differences and limitations are accepted in a non-judgemental way, then they, too, may find that they can begin to accept themselves more.

PART V

VIEWS FROM ELSEWHERE

It has been said that psychoanalytic thinking and practice is unscientific. The first chapter in this section demonstrates how conventional science can investigate issues at the core of consultations in psychoanalytic psychotherapy—for instance, qualities of a person's internal and external relational states of mind. More than this, scientific studies point to the vital importance of psychoanalytic perspectives on personal relations for understanding psychiatric disorder. The book ends with observations on the changing social context within which psychoanalytic psychotherapy consultations are conducted.

CHAPTER 10

Research reflections

R. Peter Hobson, Matthew Patrick, Raman Kapur,
& Karlen Lyons-Ruth

We intend two meanings by the title of this chapter. First, we hope to illustrate how formal, quantitative research may help us to think about issues germane to consultations in psychoanalytic psychotherapy. In particular, we shall consider the nature of transference interpretations, the distinction between paranoid-schizoid and depressive-position functioning, the qualities of certain "internal" relational states, the potential of non–transference-focused interviews or questionnaires to convey psychodynamically relevant information, and the translation from what is internal to what is external. Second, we raise some methodological issues and offer reflections on what research can and cannot achieve for a psychotherapist.

There are many people who think that psychoanalytic propositions lack scientific credibility. Yet psychoanalytic psychotherapists suppose they are dealing with facts of mental life. If the facts are indeed facts, then they might be expected to show themselves, either directly or indirectly, in phenomena amenable to measurement by non-psychoanalytic methods. These methods may not be especially sensitive from a psychoanalytic viewpoint, yet they may still reveal things that are difficult or impossible to pinpoint within the confines of the consulting room.

There will be psychotherapists who face the prospect of this chapter with ill-founded optimism, and others with resolute scepticism. We trust that what follows might temper each of these attitudes. The returns from *particular* research studies are often modest and questionable. Over time, however, research findings can gather impressive intellectual and political power. Rarely does formal research uncover startling new facts, but it can set what is partly known in a new light. That is no small accomplishment.

Finally, by way of introduction, we make a methodological point. As we hope to demonstrate, there are opportunities to be creative in studying phenomena that are relevant for psychoanalytic psychotherapy. In particular, there appears to be untapped potential in establishing how independent experts are able to converge in making reliable, objective judgements of *subjectively apprehended* patterns of interpersonal relations and communication. Provided that investigators free themselves from the straitjacket of trying to prove things, and instead engage in the serious playfulness of trying to net some important but elusive matters of fact in the psychological domain, then there may be some surprising insights to be gained from formal research.

We begin with a study of transference interpretations.

On working in the transference

One of the central claims of this book is that in assessment consultations, as in psychoanalytic psychotherapy per se, there is much to be gained from working in the transference. The transference is what a patient brings to, and relives in, his or her relationship with the therapist. For a therapist to work in the transference means that he or she attends to, and where appropriate comments upon, these patterns of relatedness.

If this sounds straightforward, it belies how much can lie buried in a simple formulation. For instance, a therapist needs to reflect upon, digest, and contain his or her countertransference feelings. Often this is an emotional necessity if the therapist's interventions, and more specifically interpretations, are to be appropriate to the patient's needs and state of mind at any moment. Moreover, as we saw in chapter 7, different therapists conceptualize their task of analysing and interpreting the transference in rather different ways.

A substantial part of this book has been concerned with a relatively direct, eyeball-to-eyeball, here-and-now mode of psychotherapy consultation. At various points, however, the potential value of alternative approaches has been acknowledged. One might reasonably enquire, what *are* the contrasts among different styles of psychoanalytic psychotherapy? How should we think about, and if possible study, divergences in clinical practice?

The following study (Hobson & Kapur, 2005, which is related to Kapur's 1998 doctoral thesis on the operationalization of Kleinian concepts) concerns what psychoanalytic psychotherapists say and do in consultations or therapy sessions. It addresses just a few of the many features of psychotherapeutic technique that vary from one psychotherapist to another. We selected a seemingly narrow focus—namely, the content of different therapists' interpretations. Our aim was not only to home in on some specifics of practice, but also to see how far differences in styles of interpreting reflect wide-ranging differences in therapeutic technique. This might help us to reflect on what we are doing, and what we might choose to change in what we are doing, when conducting psychotherapy consultations.

By and large, psychotherapy researchers who study transference interpretations give few *examples* of what they are actually studying. There are exceptions, though. For example, Hoglend et al. (2006) offer the following as a prototypical example of a transference interpretation:

> You told me that your colleague is doing less than her share of the job, which led to a headache that has bothered you since our last session. Could this perhaps also be related to a feeling you have that I do not do my share of the therapeutic work? It may be difficult to say this directly to me. [p. 1740].

(Hoglend et al. give further examples on p. 1744.) With this interpretation in mind, consider three dimensions on which psychotherapists can differ in making transference interpretations:

1. The degree to which the interpretations are anchored in (and often restricted to) the immediate here-and-now interactions

between patient and therapist. Alternatively, interpretations may entail more abstract (there-and-then) reflection on the determinants of the patient's experience and characteristics. Often related to this dimension of immediacy is how far a therapist deems it appropriate to interpret patterns of relatedness early and frequently in sessions, or to wait until the nature of historical links become evident.

2. The degree to which interpretations are intended not only to capture a patient's emotional conflicts felt in relation to the psychotherapist, but also to highlight what the patient is *doing* (consciously or unconsciously) to him/herself and the psychotherapist, in order to shape the emotional interaction and retain psychological equilibrium.

3. The degree to which the interpretations are framed as a more or less explicit invitation for the patient to consider possible meanings in a conversation with the psychotherapist.

In conducting our study, we were grateful to two research groups, one from Canada led by Bill Piper (e.g., Piper, Azim, Joyce, & McCallum, 1991), and the other from the US made up of Connolly, Crits-Christoph, and Luborsky (e.g., Connolly et al., 1999). These researchers very kindly provided us with examples of therapist interventions that satisfied their own definitions of transference interpretations. We shall not dwell on the definitions per se but, rather, illustrate what they appear to mean in practice. Our own material came from three videotapes of assessment consultations conducted by the first author (PH) in the course of routine NHS practice in an outpatient psychotherapy clinic.

Our first, informal approach was to compare specific instances of transference interpretations provided by the three research groups. The following comprise single, more or less typical, examples from each group. We begin with an interpretation provided by Connolly (personal communication, February 2002):

> Sounds like you, if, you know, people at home would start to help more, maybe, maybe you could breathe, but it's hard for you to just take the initiative. . . . I was wondering about that here too, whether or not that might be the issue here, that you'd rather I took the lead.

As it happens, the content as well as style of this interpretation is similar to that of Hoglend given earlier. Together, the quotations serve both to convey a particular way of inviting a patient to reflect on what is happening in relation to the therapist, and to link this with the patient's reports of his or her relationships in everyday life.

The following example from Piper has a different tone and orientation:

> I think it would seem like you're trying to preserve some part of your experience of me. And the way you're trying to do that is to keep your irritability, your anger, your frustration, your anxiety back out so that it doesn't threaten to come in and destroy everything.

When we turn to our own transcripts, we need to clarify our use of terms if subsequent results from the study are to make sense. We defined an "interpretation" as a comment by the therapist aimed to clarify the meaning(s) of the patient–therapist interaction that had just taken place. An "in-transference interpretation" comprised a therapist statement or group of statements that contained specific and direct reference to the therapist, usually containing the word "I" or "me", intended to clarify the patient's current feelings or actions in relation to the therapist. Here is an in-transference interpretation (a rather long one) from our transcripts (additional ones appear in Hobson and Kapur, 2005):

> You see I think this goes very deep, in the questionnaire two of the things you mentioned, one was at one phase you had a, I don't know, a true problem with eating but also you said something about this peculiar business of sleeping a lot. At any moment in this contact between you and I, I'm not at all clear what you're taking in from me and what you're not. I'm not at all clear what you're asleep to or what you're awake to. There seems to be something that registers with you and then it seems lost, what I call a kind of deadening, as if you can resolve without really thinking about it, or that you kind-of take in but don't really make your own, you don't really assimilate it, you don't really take in.

We hope that potential contrasts among styles of interpretation have become self-evident from these brief illustrations. Now we focus on in-transference interpretations from our own study

(Hobson & Kapur, 2005). This book contains many other instances of interventions made by the psychotherapist (PH), and these, too, can be evaluated according to the conceptual scheme we introduce here.

In relation to the in-transference interpretations recorded in the study, it seemed to our (not entirely objective) eyes that three qualities stood out. First, most in-transference interpretations seemed to be anchored in the immediate here-and-now of the patient–therapist exchanges. They tended to be specific to what had just happened or was happening, and although they occasionally made reference to links with other relationships or with recurrent patterns of relating ("in the questionnaire two of the things you mentioned . . ."), these instances were immediately followed by reference to current transactions. The in-transference interpretations were essentially local and tightly focused, rather than general or abstract.

Second, in-transference interpretations were centred on how the patient experienced the therapist, including qualities of anxiety and defence; on the patient's focus of attention, including what the therapist was thinking or doing; and on what the patient was trying to *do*. This "doing" was sometimes framed in terms of the patient's attempts to deal with his or her own mental states ("There seems to be something that registers with you and it then seems lost, what I call a kind of deadening", ". . . you kind-of take in but don't really make your own"), but more often in terms of how the patient was attempting to configure the interaction with the therapist. Often the interpretation referred to how the patient was manoeuvring the therapist to feel certain things or to adopt a prescribed role within the exchange. This kind of interpretative work gave emphasis to how the patient dealt with the therapist's own stance and, in particular, to the ways the patient experienced and used what the therapist offered by way of statements that were intended to express understanding.

Third, the style of interpretation was direct, in the sense that often the therapist did not explicitly invite the patient to reflect with him on his observations or conjectures. Instead he articulated what he believed he was witnessing on the basis of evidence that was also available to the patient (and which therefore could be disputed). Obviously, he was also presenting his observations so that the patient could make use of them, and, as we have seen, he paid close attention to the patient's reactions. Having said this, a substantial number of the therapist's interventions began with "You see . . .", or "I think . . .", and this conveyed how he was putting a viewpoint that he hoped the patient might understand or at least consider. This last finding came as something of a surprise to the therapist.

A second aim of the Hobson and Kapur (2005) study was to establish whether independent raters could agree over instances of in-transference interpretation, and, if they could, how frequently such interpretations occurred. On a five-point scale, two independent judges showed substantial agreement in rating the "in-transference-quality" of the therapist's interpretations. When we computed the proportion of paired judgements that were within one point of each other, 85.4% of ratings met this criterion. We adopted the criterion that only those interpretations that were given scores of 5 or 4 (as agreed between the two judges in a final, joint rating) would count as in-transference interpretations.

It turned out that the therapist (PH) gave strikingly more frequent transference interpretations than reported by any previous study. Over the first 50 minutes of three separate assessment consultations, he made between 18 and 24 transference interpretations. This compares with a mean of 5 transference interpretations per routine psychotherapy session recorded by Piper et al. (1991), the 1 to 3 transference interpretations considered to represent "moderate frequency" by Hoglend et al. (2006), and fewer than one per cent of therapist statements reported by Connolly et al. (1999).

The findings indicate that in the first two-thirds of the consultations, covering a period of approximately 50 minutes in each, the psychotherapist was making a substantial number of interpretations—that is, statements exploring the meaning of what the patient was doing or saying. Interpretations came thick and fast. Between one-third and three-fifths of these were in-transference interpretations. In the period studied for each of the three patients, the therapist gave in-transference interpretations at an average rate of one every 2 to 3 minutes.

The "average rate" does not mean very much, because of uneven distribution over time. It was mostly the case that in-transference interpretations were prevalent in the first phase of the interview, when the therapist was attempting to involve the patient in clarifying and understanding what was happening in the therapeutic encounter. Then there were dense but somewhat patchy periods of in-transference interpretations in the second phase of the interviews, and, in one case, a further burst at the end. Here one should recall how patients differ in the degree to which "hot" and perceptible transference-related material emerges quickly or more gradually. Sometimes the transference is clarified only when aspects of the patient's history crystallize and give shape to preliminary indications of relationship patterns.

If we return to consider contrasts among therapists, it is important to remember that only in our own study were transcripts taken from assessment consultations. Moreover, the interviews were structured in a way that highlighted patients' propensities to experience and deal with an *initially* inscrutable therapist. It required the therapist to provide active input in helping the patient to understand and manage this specifically interpersonal field of transaction. No wonder that such work was focused on the patient's relation to the therapist. And no wonder that the therapist was especially attentive to how the patient *acted* upon and then *used* the therapist's own state of mind and interpretive interventions. These became the "hot" issues in the immediate here-and-now.

This research was preliminary and was confined to material from very small numbers of therapists and patients. Yet it illustrates how the focus and conduct of psychodynamic psychotherapy—reflected in, but by no means confined to, the therapist's interpretations—can vary markedly from one psychotherapist to another. Although there are sceptics who believe that differences among supposedly distinct forms of psychotherapy are trivial, this does not *seem* to be the case, even within the sub-domain of psychoanalytic psychotherapy. Here we find that psychotherapists' interventions may show substantial differences in style, rather as classical music contrasts with jazz.

There is, of course, a place for classical music and a place for jazz—it is just that they are not the same. When contemplating the nature and practice of psychoanalytic psychotherapy, including assessment consultations, this is important to bear in mind. A therapist has options in how he or she conducts a consultation.

Alternative ways of approaching the task of consultation may have implications for what a consultation reveals, and what development the consultation promotes, for any given patient.

From a complementary perspective, our study bears upon the interpretation of others' research. In particular, the *meaning* of measures of frequency of transference interpretation can be evaluated only within the framework of the total therapeutic situation. Highly discrepant frequencies of interpretation across therapists make sense only once they are seen to reflect different modes of working in the transference. Despite what might be deduced from the research of others, one cannot prescribe "doses" of transference interpretation as if one were prescribing doses of medication. More generally—and importantly—any research into psychoanalytic psychotherapy needs to take variability into account. In relation to certain research questions, between-therapist as well as between-patient variability may matter relatively little. For other intents and purposes, it is likely to matter a great deal.

Relational patterns in the transference

Central to the theory of psychoanalytic psychotherapy are two ideas: first, that a person repeats patterns of interpersonal relations; and second, that such patterns are discernible (and potentially accessible to influence) in the transference. Some modes of interpersonal relatedness are more "primitive" and less integrated than others. It is often important to determine a patient's level of functioning, and one can make mistakes in this regard. One approach to characterizing different forms of mental organization originates in the work of Melanie Klein (1935, 1946), who contrasted paranoid-schizoid states of mind with those that characterize the depressive position. How might one study the relevance of a Kleinian perspective for consultations in psychoanalytic psychotherapy— and beyond this, its relevance for understanding certain psychiatric disorders?

In undertaking the following study (Hobson, Patrick, & Valentine, 1998), we harboured political as well as scientific motives.

Sure enough, we were interested in discovering something about certain classes of patient and the nature of their engagements with a psychoanalytic psychotherapist. Perhaps more centrally, we were interested in exploring the application of a novel methodology to phenomena that had not been subject to quantitative research. We felt optimistic that conventional scientific methods applied to appropriate clinical material could reach into parts of the mind that had so far eluded measurement. For decades, the modes of psychological function in question had featured prominently in psychoanalytic theories. Outside psychoanalysis, critics had dismissed these accounts as "purely subjective" in status.

A third motive, related to the first two but rather different in kind, was to see if we could publish the study in a mainstream psychiatric journal. This might prompt psychiatrists and psychologists to re-examine some of their prejudices about psychoanalytic accounts of relational patterns seen in troubled patients.

With this last aim in mind, we needed to ensure that our methodological approach dovetailed with—as well as offered a challenge to—conventional psychiatric thinking. So we decided to study adult females with borderline personality disorder (BPD). Here was a diagnosis enshrined in the *Diagnostic and Statistical Manual* of the American Psychiatric Association (*DSM–III-R*; APA, 1987—the version employed at the time of our studies), and one that lent itself to psychoanalytically orientated study. Our hypothesis was that the coherence of the syndrome of BPD reflects the "object relational" (interpersonal) structures of experience and defence that characterize affected individuals. In other words, what psychiatrists have identified as BPD, we view as a relatively pure culture of individuals who tend to manifest primitive states of mental organization.

From a psychiatric perspective, then, what *is* the syndrome of BPD? And from a psychoanalytic viewpoint, what *are* these primitive relational states? Answers to these questions are needed before one can study the degree of fit between diagnosis and proposed relational configurations.

Individuals are said to have the syndrome of BPD when they meet five out of nine diagnostic criteria: a pattern of intense, unstable relationships; impulsiveness in at least two areas that are potentially self-damaging; affective instability; inappropriate, intense anger or lack of control of anger; recurrent suicidal threats or self-mutilating behaviour; marked and persistent identity disturbance; chronic feelings of emptiness or boredom; frantic efforts to avoid real or imagined abandonment; and transient paranoid or dissociative symptoms.

Here we offer a brief aside. It is far from self-evident that, defined in this way, the syndrome of BPD should be associated with particular forms of self–other experience and/or mental representation. Indeed, many psychiatrists and psychologists would dispute that it is. Many more would baulk at the idea that relational patterns and forms of dynamic organization are *basic* to the syndrome. Our aim was to take a scientific look, to see whether a proposal like this has more plausibility than some might think.

We selected cases from a collection of videotaped assessment consultations conducted by one of us (PH) as part of routine NHS practice. Seven videotapes depicted patients with BPD, and seven featured patients with dysthymia (a depression of mood lasting at least two years but without evidence of major depressive disorder). We invited six psychodynamically trained psychotherapists to watch the first 30 minutes of these 14 videotaped assessment interviews. Their task was to make ratings of the qualities of interpersonal relatedness between each patient and PH as therapist, according to a 30-item "personal relatedness profile".

In the personal relatedness profile, which appears in full in the original publication (Hobson, Patrick, & Valentine, 1998), we tried to capture the essence of paranoid-schizoid and depressive-position functioning. The focus was not on the operation of mental mechanisms such as splitting, denial, and projective identification, which have been posited to shape more primitive states of mind, but on manifest relational patterns. In fact, we allowed raters to take into account both relatedness as witnessed in a patient's relation with the therapist, and relatedness as described by the patient with reference to everyday relationships.

The first part of the profile focuses on personal relatedness, the second on the characteristics of the people ("objects") experienced or described, and the third (which we came to see as subsidiary) on the patient's predominant affective states. Each part has 10 items, half of which are intended to characterize paranoid-schizoid functioning, and half depressive-position functioning. They are scored between 1 and 5 for being (un)characteristic of a given patient. By way of illustration, below are some the items (P-S stands for paranoid-schizoid, DP for depressive position):

Characteristic "relatedness patterns" in which the patient is implicated:

» Mutuality involving freedom for (and potentially loving links between) participants (DP)

» Vengefulness, retaliation, operating by the "law of talion" (P-S)

» Lack of concern, use of people as things (P-S)

» Clear or subtle indications of locked-in hostility, abuse, victimization, and/or controlled/controlling relations (including sadomasochism) (P-S)

» A capacity for ambivalence, in which the patient (or other people described) grapple with the complexities of relationships (DP)

Characteristics of people ("objects") as experienced by the patient:

» Loyal, committed, "straight" (DP)

» Narcissistic, self-preoccupied, unattuned, using others for self-gratification (P-S)

» Emotionally available and caring, with recognition of the needs and wishes of others (DP)

» Able to acknowledge dependence and helplessness without overwhelming anxiety, possibly genuinely grateful (DP)

» Persecutory, dreadful, malevolent, gratuitously nasty (P-S)

So what happened when psychotherapists watched the fourteen 30-minute videotapes of the assessment consultations and rated what they saw on items such as these?

The first result was that independent raters showed substantial agreement in their judgements of the items in the personal relatedness profile. A given patient's patterns of interpersonal relatedness, and the characteristics of the people (including the therapist) experienced by the patient, could be identified in an "objective" way. The specifically psychoanalytic descriptions were not merely "subjective" in the sense of being idiosyncratic or imagined—they captured something objective about patients' interpersonal relations.

Second, the intercorrelations among item scores were most plausibly explained by a single factor that corresponded with the distinction between paranoid-schizoid and depressive-position functioning. In other words, individuals who scored highly for paranoid-schizoid items were also likely to score highly on other items of this kind, whereas those who scored highly for depressive-position items were also relatively consistent across items.

Finally, when the ill-fitting items were excluded and we examined how individual patients scored on the scale, we were impressed to find that there was an almost complete division between the two diagnostic groups. Sure enough, the scores of the dysthymic patients indicated a fair amount of paranoid-schizoid functioning, as one would expect, and there was a slim area of overlap. Yet even with such small numbers of patients in each group, there was a very clear and statistically significant group difference. Almost all the women with BPD scored more highly for paranoid-schizoid functioning, and lower for depressive position functioning, than almost all the women with dysthymia.

Therefore, it turned out that there was a remarkably close link between diagnosis and our measures of psychoanalytically conceived relational states. This does not establish that troubled relational states are what *underlie* the manifold psychiatric/descriptive features of BPD, of course, but certainly it is compatible with such a claim. Moreover, any account of the disorder needs to explain how such relational patterns figure so consistently in the clinical picture. These patients' emotional difficulties, although sometimes portrayed by psychiatrists as disorders of mood, comprised emotionally charged *personal relations* of relatively specific kinds. What are abstracted as "affective instability" or "intense anger" in the criteria for BPD are just that—abstracted from the interpersonal dynamics of which these emotional features are aspects.

It may be worth highlighting how this study achieved what it did. We were careful to choose our groups so that they differed *both* in psychiatric diagnosis *and* (according to our hypothesis) in psychoanalytic characteristics. The clinical material was selected from consultations that were designed to highlight individual differences in the states of mind we were studying. We devised a measure that was close to psychoanalytic thinking and, at the same time, focused on what psychodynamically trained judges could observe in videotaped patient–therapist interactions. We checked whether independent raters who were unaware of patient diagnoses could agree in their judgements on our measure. We made a prediction about a group difference that would be apparent when the data were analysed.

With all these design features in place, the study was ready to launch. Perhaps most critical was our decision to measure qualities of interpersonal engagement through trained professionals working with a sufficiently sophisticated and sensitive rating scale. The results surprised even ourselves.

"Internal" relational states

Another core feature of psychoanalytic thinking is that there is constant interplay between relations that are external, in the sense of being lived out with others, and those that are internal, in the sense of being represented and lived out within an individual's mind. In the following collaborative study (Lyons-Ruth, Melnick, Patrick, & Hobson, 2007), again of adults with BPD, we flipped to the "internal" side of the coin.

We focused on hostile and helpless states of mind in women with BPD. Our participants were 12 women with this diagnosis, and 11 women with dysthymia who were similar in age, diagnostic status, and ratings on a measure of depression. This time we studied not videotapes but transcripts from interviews concerned with significant early relationships, the Adult Attachment Interview (AAI; George, Kaplan, & Main, 1985). We describe this interview at greater length in the next section, but suffice it to say that the person interviewed reflects on his or her early significant relationships and experiences, especially those (including separation, upset, or trauma) in relation to attachment figures.

We employed a rating scale for the AAI designed by Karlen Lyons-Ruth and colleagues, the Hostile-Helpless Coding System (Lyons-Ruth, Yellin, Melnick, & Atwood, 2005). This is made up of a number of indicators that contribute to an overall scaled score (range 1–9) for level of Hostile-Helpless state of mind, as follows:

» Frequency of global devaluation of a caregiver, including actively negative devaluation and "cool" derogating descriptions

» identification with a devalued caregiver, where a participant appears to value or accept similarities between the negatively evaluated attachment figure and the self, even though these similarities may not be explicitly acknowledged

» Recurrent references to fearful affect

» Recurrent references to a sense of self as bad, including feelings of guilt and responsibility, and of deserving disrespect or being undeserving of positive attention

» Recurrent instances of laughter at pain, in which the relating of emotionally painful or negative experiences is accompanied by laughter

» Ruptured attachments, when a participant refers to no longer having contact with one or more nuclear family members through a deliberate decision to terminate contact.

One statement scoring high for global devaluation of a caregiver was: "I even feel contempt. I don't hate them any more, I used to hate them, I used to daydream what I'd do to them, how I'd kill them, but she is not worth it." A statement reflecting identification with a devalued caregiver was: ". . . and I used to shout at them in the same way that people I felt threatened by used to tell me off like school teachers and things, and my mother. I use the same tone and say the same sort of things." Here one sees how the patient feels caught up in enacting towards others just "the same sort of [threatening] things" that she felt her mother displayed towards herself.

Individuals are classified as having a Hostile-Helpless state of mind regarding important attachment experiences if they score

5 or above on the overall scale. Transcripts classified as Hostile-Helpless are characterized by evidence of opposing evaluations of central relationships occurring across the interview that are neither discussed nor reconciled by the participant—for example, "We were friends . . . We were enemies". It will be clear how closely this scheme aligns with psychoanalytic theorizing.

In keeping with three hierarchical (non-independent) *a priori* predictions, the results were that (1) all patients with BPD, compared with half the group with dysthymia, displayed Hostile-Helpless states of mind; (2) those with BPD manifested a significantly higher frequency of globally devaluing representations; and (3) those with BPD exhibited a strong trend towards identifying with the devalued hostile caregiver (58% borderline vs. 18% dysthymic). In addition, significantly more borderline than dysthymic patients made reference to controlling behaviour towards attachment figures in childhood.

Here once again we find that formal research methods *of the appropriate kind* may promote a shift in theoretical orientation towards relational processes—internal as well as external—as critical for, or at least characteristic of, individuals with particular forms of personality disorder. In picking out specific features of psychodynamic psychopathology for appraisal, and examining these in the context of comparisons between groups of patients with relevant forms of psychiatric disorder, one can reveal things that might otherwise remain obscure. What consultations can do for the individual patient, formal research can sometimes achieve for the nature of psychopathology.

"Mental representations" of relationships

Psychoanalysts have elaborated on the connection between the qualities of a person's interpersonal relations and his or her capacity to think. One manifestation of thinking is a person's discourse. In chapter 4, it was noted how some patients' questionnaires contain scant information, others are filled out in capital letters, others are crammed full of scrawled detail. Almost always, such individual differences turn out to express a person's emotional/relational difficulties, albeit in ways that may become apparent only when the consultation has been conducted.

Recent research in the attachment tradition has explored this link between relationships and thinking. Some years ago, we decided to adopt what was then a novel measure, the AAI (George, Kaplan, & Main, 1985), to explore thinking and discourse among individuals with BPD (Patrick, Hobson, Castle, Howard, & Maughan, 1994). The reason we did so, was that we considered this measure to be a scientifically tractable index of psychodynamic organization.

We need to say something further about the AAI itself. One important thing to bear in mind is how the Interview was derived. In the mid-1980s, Mary Main and colleagues had at their disposal a group of over 40 parents (mainly mothers) who had been tested with their infants five years earlier to assess the infants' reactions to separation from their parent (George, Kaplan & Main, 1985). What the investigators did was to interview the parents and see if there were any correspondences between the mother–infant separation–reunion reactions five years earlier and the ways the mothers were now able to think and talk about their own childhood experiences. This was a really clever idea. In effect, the infants were being used as an index of the mother–infant relationship, and that relationship was being used to discriminate one kind of maternal interview from another. It turned out that most mothers in "secure" mother–infant relationships were "free to evaluate" their own childhoods, whereas "insecure" mother–infant relationships were those that involved mothers who tended to be either dismissive in their attitudes to their own childhoods or entangled or enmeshed in their accounts of their early relationships.

In other words, relationships *as observed* between mothers and their infants corresponded with the coherence with which mothers could *think about* their own early relationships.

Especially important for the present purposes is when a person manifests an enmeshed state of mind. This tends to result in a long interview (as in an overflowing questionnaire). The person's discourse shows unexplained oscillations of viewpoint, tangential or irrelevant responses, and highly entangled, confused, run-on sentences. Here, by way of illustration, is part of one transcript from someone with BPD:

> "Um, I felt closer to my mother, um, because she made me feel special, I think—that uh, that anything was possible and that I was going to do really well and uh, everything would be ok. Um, it was quite a nice feeling to have and it was quite different from my father's—the only thing that I got from my father which was like, you were going to be ok and things would . . . there would always be blocks in my way and things would . . . there would always be blocks in my way and one would always be infinitely disappointed by life . . ."

An additional rating of the interview concerns cognitive disorganization and/or disorientation when the person talks about experiences of loss or trauma. The signs include lapses in reasoning or unfounded fear or guilt, or irrational thought processes when the individual is talking about these topics. When such features are present, the person is said to be "unresolved" with respect to loss and/or trauma.

Our own hypotheses about the functioning of patients with BPD derived from psychoanalytic developmental theory. We drew upon the ideas of Bion (1962), who argued that a young child requires a sufficiently sensitive and emotionally containing caregiver if he or she is to develop the capacities to contain and assimilate experiences and feelings and to think effectively. If there is no sensitive caregiver available, then the child may be unable to integrate difficult or traumatic interpersonal events. We considered that patients with BPD form a relatively homogeneous group precisely because they have difficulty in containing difficult feelings and deploy characteristic, cognitively disruptive defences as a result.

Once again we were treating the psychiatric diagnosis of BPD as a means to constitute a group that we anticipated would be relatively homogeneous in their defensive styles and mental organization. We predicted that when compared with patients with dysthymia, they would be more likely to (1) come out as "enmeshed" in the AAI, and (2) show evidence of being "unresolved/ disorganized" in relation to traumatic happenings in their childhoods.

Our participants were 12 borderline and 12 dysthymic female patients from the psychotherapy waiting list. These were more or less the same groups as were involved in the Hostile-Helpless study described earlier. The interview transcripts were rated by someone who was unaware of the nature of the study and of the patient groups.

Remarkably, all 12 of the borderline patients but only 4 of the dysthymic patients were rated as preoccupied/enmeshed on the AAI (for similar but less black-and-white results, see Fonagy et al., 1996). Indeed, 10 of the 12 borderline and none of the dysthymic women were classified into one particular subcategory, E3, meaning that they appeared "confused, fearful and overwhelmed" in relation to experiences with attachment figures.

In addition, although the overall rates of trauma and loss were very similar in the two groups, with 9 out of 12 borderline subjects and 10 out of 12 dysthymic subjects reporting episodes that met the criteria for significant trauma or loss set out in the AAI rating schedule, all 9 of the borderline subjects were classified as unresolved with respect to the trauma or loss they reported, compared with only 2 of the 10 dysthymic patients. When we focused more specifically on trauma, we found that 6 borderline patients reported such experiences, ranging from frightening beatings to childhood sexual abuse. Five patients from our dysthymic group reported traumata of comparable severity. However, all 6 of the borderline patients were classified as unresolved with respect to these traumatic experiences, whereas none of the 5 dysthymic patients were classified in this way. Only the latter, non-borderline women could think about their experiences coherently.

What this meant was that patients with the largely *behaviourally* defined syndrome of BPD had a distinctive pattern of *mental organization* that conformed with what we anticipated on the basis of psychoanalytic theory. The results point to the need to consider how individuals with BPD come to think (or not-think) in the ways that they do, and to consider further the *development* of thinking in the context of their intersubjective experiences in past and present intimate relationships. The way is open to integrate the present results with those from the studies already cited on paranoid-schizoid functioning and Hostile-Helpless relational states among borderline individuals.

Back to the external

We can add a final piece of research to complement what has gone before. If the psychoanalytic view is correct, and what is internal becomes lived out in intimate relationships, then how might one expect mothers with BPD to relate to their infants?

Crandell, Patrick, and Hobson (2003) studied mothers with BPD in face-to-face play with their 2-month-old infants. The mothers tended to be rated as "intrusively insensitive". In response to the mother assuming a "still face" for 90 seconds, infants of these mothers showed more dazed looks and more looks away from the mother than did infants of non-borderline mothers, and they were relatively depressed in mood subsequently. This striking finding suggests that as early as 2 months of age, the infants of borderline mothers were less able to manage the challenge of relating to an unresponsive mother. Some people who watched the videotapes wondered if the infants felt "paranoid". Potentially untoward implications for the infants' subsequent development were evident when they reached 12 months of age (Hobson, Patrick, Crandell, García-Pérez, & Lee, 2005). In particular, a large majority showed disorganized attachment patterns.

In the latter, follow-up study (Hobson et al., 2005), this time in a teaching task, borderline mothers were again rated as intrusively insensitive towards their infants. Subsequent research involved more subtle ratings of maternal behaviour as applied to mother–infant separation–reunion episodes (Hobson et al., 2009). Compared with mothers with depression or without psychopathology, a higher proportion (85%) of women with BPD showed disrupted affective communication with their infants. They were especially distinguished by the prevalence of frightened/disoriented behaviour, a pattern strongly associated with infant disorganized attachment (Hesse & Main, 2006).

The take-home message is that relational patterns constitute deeply embedded aspects of psychopathology. One implication is that there may be serious risk of the cross-generational transmission of disorder. This, too, may be a concern that arises in psychotherapy consultations.

Final reflections

How might this research be of value to the psychoanalytic psychotherapist who conducts assessment consultations? We leave it to you, our readers, to judge whether your views on the nature and conceptual focus of consultations in psychoanalytic psychotherapy, and the nature and implications of serious psychopathology, have been enriched, challenged, or otherwise altered by the studies we have described. One way to think about this is to ask: "Would I have predicted the findings in advance of knowing the results?"

We finish with a different kind of reflection. The studies described in this chapter provide an unusual *form* of empirical support for the view that when someone seeks psychiatric or psychological help, then a systematic and disciplined exploration of the person's relational patterns may be important. Moreover, it would appear that a certain style of assessing—and more than this, a certain way of seeing and interpreting clinical phenomena—may need to be brought to bear if a consultation is going to capture critical aspects of a person's emotional difficulties. Mainstream psychiatry and psychology do not have the wherewithal to achieve the *particular* forms of insight that psychoanalytic consultations can deliver. Such insights cannot be dismissed as marginal to clinical appraisal and management. They may be of central significance for understanding a person's psychiatric disorder and of pivotal importance for deciding on appropriate intervention.

CHAPTER 11

Afterthoughts

Antony Garelick

My contribution is going to be brief. In early chapters of this volume, Ruth Berkowitz and Jane Milton kindly made reference to a paper I published in 1994, entitled "Psychotherapy Assessment: Theory and Practice". Here I offer some reflections on what has changed since I wrote that paper. What I say will complement the many important issues raised and discussed by other contributors to this volume.

The unconscious is timeless. The ways in which patients present may alter over time—for instance, classic conversion hysteria seems to have given way to medically unexplained symptoms and psychosomatic disorders—but people's underlying conflicts and emotional difficulties probably remain much the same. What changes more rapidly are society and the environment within which psychoanalytic psychotherapy is delivered.

Consider the changing relationship between patient and psychoanalytic psychotherapist. Twenty years ago the authority of the practitioner was not questioned. Services were paternalistic in nature. By and large, patients did not challenge the status of the consultant psychotherapist, nor make discomforting demands. They were being assessed, not consulted. The question was whether or not they were suitable for a particular modality of treatment.

Patients' expectations have changed. Now the consumer rules. As often as not, patients are no longer called patients. They have rights, entitlements, and access to more information. They need to give informed consent. They require everything to be more explicit. They have the right to know just about everything and to have access to professional letters and documents.

Correspondingly, psychotherapy consultation has become a subtle negotiation. The question now is which treatment might be more suitable for, and most acceptable to, a given patient.

Of course, much of this is to the good. But change brings unintended consequences.

What flexibility remains for the conduct of an analytic consultation? Suppose that for a period a therapist remains relatively silent, working on the principle that free association may be most effective for exploring and coming to understand a person's underlying state of mind. In the present climate, this represents a stark deviation from what a patient expects, and from what many patients feel entitled to expect. Some would take the view that any variation away from the customary transaction between patient and doctor, such as taking a history, asking specific questions, and prescribing treatment, has to be explained prior to the consultation. Is this, too, as it should be? What costs as well as benefits arise from this practice? Or, from a complementary perspective, at what risk does the psychoanalytic psychotherapist undertake his or her work, if this needs to involve challenge and confrontation with, as well as sympathy and support for, a patient? Suppose what a patient seeks—whether to excise parts of the personality, or engage in a collusive relationship—is the last thing the patient needs?

I have highlighted potential problems. There are also the benefits. For instance, I have stressed how patients expect explicit information and a rationale for their treatment. There are healthy aspects to this. It is very important that the process of consultation makes a person more, not less, responsible for his or her life. So, too, I have been led to adjust aspects of my technique, and not merely from caution. These days, for example, I am more committed to following up whatever interpretations or interventions I make. Often it helps to make sure that these are registered and accessible to the patient in conscious, explicit form. This also provides an opportunity to gauge a patient's response when unconscious experience is transformed into verbal communication.

There have been other, related shifts in perspective. The psychotherapy market place has become crowded with a plethora of technical approaches. Mostly, these focus on what can be articulated and rendered explicit. Treatments advertise themselves as brief, and with measurable outcomes. Each of these qualities comes to be incorporated in what patients expect a treatment to deliver. No wonder if patients are dismayed by a treatment that involves disturbance or pain, and one that might prove lengthy and is not at all certain in outcome. Beyond this, psychoanalytic psychotherapy points them in the direction of what is unknown and unformulated, instead of reassuring them over what they can summarize and manage according to a Treatment Plan.

Of course, being concerned with symptom alleviation is not at all incompatible with seeking after depth of understanding. Yet medical practice in general, and styles of psychotherapy in particular, are becoming increasingly protocol-driven. This procedural approach dovetails with an evidence-based orientation, in part because the evidence needs to come from (and is applicable to) carefully standardized and monitored treatments. The evidence in question is derived from systematic, statistically analysed data pertaining to group comparisons, often comparison of groups of patients receiving different treatments.

Such evidence may have value, but it fails to encompass everything that is important. There remains much particular to an individual who seeks a consultation. Each patient has his or her own personal narrative, subjective experience, and hopes, fears, and dreams. These unique aspects of a person are not merely details to qualify the diagnoses of a "condition" such as anxiety or depression. They, too, deserve respect and therapeutic attention. Patients who are psychologically minded may be desperate to be heard and understood. The powerful experience of engaging with a psychotherapist can open up an internal dialogue within the patient's mind.

When I think about my recent clinical work with high-functioning professionals, I find that two classes of patient immediately come to mind. In many high-achieving perfectionist individuals, the predominant dynamic concerns the harsh nature of their superego, ranging from the hypercritical to the self-punitive to the ego-destructive. Invariably, this becomes expressed in the transference, where insight and some amelioration may be achieved. The second category of patients comprises those who have a discrete symptom presentation. One challenging example is body dysmorphic disorder, often amounting to a quasi-delusional state. The focus of the consultation is on shifting the patient towards a new way of understanding his or her symptoms. Given time, even in the face of denial and disavowal, some patients can begin to grasp that emotional difficulties have been projected into their bodies. Then a more creative dialogue can develop. It is difficult to see how non-psychoanalytic forms of psychological intervention would result in these particular kinds of developmental progress.

In summary, changes in society and the environment have profound implications for the management of consultations in psychoanalytic psychotherapy. If, according to a consumerist model, psychotherapy is but one class of material goods, then should we be packaging and marketing our product to make the consumer happy? What is the alternative? How might one devote serious attention to unconscious factors such as those revealed in the transference and countertransference, while responding to societal and institutional demands and expectations?

It would seem there is a need to formulate, and perhaps reformulate, what the enterprise is about. The essence of psycho-analytic psychotherapy remains the same—that is, to enable patients to make sense of what is happening in their lives, from emotional, developmental, and relationship-orientated points of view. The aim is to bring greater understanding to bear on the person's difficulties and, with this, help the patient achieve greater integration in his or her mind and life. If one can make hitherto unconscious phenomena conscious, and by doing so enable the healthy part of the ego to utilize new insights and awareness in the service of greater control and choice, then a patient may be set free from the grip of repetitive, unconscious, and maladaptive intrapsychic and interpersonal transactions and come to feel more empowered as a person.

REFERENCES

Aarons, Z. A. (1962). Indications for analysis and problems of analyzability. *Psychoanalytic Quarterly, 31:* 514–531.

Abraham, K. (1919). The applicability of psychoanalytic therapy to patients of advanced age. In: *Selected Papers on Psycho-Analysis* (pp. 312–317). London: Hogarth Press [reprinted London: Karnac, 1979].

APA (1987). *Diagnostic and Statistical Manual of Mental Disorders* (3rd edition, revised). Washington, DC: American Psychiatric Association.

Bachrach, H. M., & Leaff, L. (1978). Analysability: A systematic review of the clinical and quantitative literature. *Journal of the American Psychoanalytic Association, 26:* 881–920.

Bachrach, H. M., Weber, J., & Solomon, M. (1985). Factors associated with the outcome of psychoanalysis (clinical and methodological considerations): Report of the Columbia Psychoanalytic Center Research Project IV. *International Review of Psychoanalysis, 12:* 379–389.

Baker, R. (1980). The finding of "not suitable" in the selection of supervised cases. *International Review of Psychoanalysis, 7:* 353–364.

Bibring, F. (1937). Symposium on the theory of the therapeutic results of psycho-analysis. *International Journal of Psychoanalysis, 18:* 170–189.

Bion, W. R. (1962). A theory of thinking. *International Journal of Psychoanalysis, 43:* 306–310.

Bloch, S. (1979). Assessment of patients for psychotherapy. *British Journal of Psychiatry, 135:* 193–208.

Britton, R. (1998). *Belief and Imagination: Explorations in Psychoanalysis*. London: Routledge.

Coltart, N. (1987). Diagnosis and assessment of suitability for psychoanalytic psychotherapy. In: *Slouching Towards Bethlehem and Further Psychoanalytic Explorations* (pp. 15–26). London: Free Association Books, 1992.

Connolly, M. B., Crits-Christoph, P., Shappell, S., Barber, J. P., Luborsky, L., & Shaffer, C. (1999). Relation of transference interpretations to outcome in the early sessions of brief supportive-expressive psychotherapy. *Psychotherapy Research, 9:* 485–495.

Cooper, J., & Alfillé, H. (Eds.) (1998). *Assessment in Psychotherapy*. London: Karnac, 2005.

Crandell, L. E., Patrick, M. P. H., & Hobson, R. P. (2003). "Still-face" interactions between mothers with borderline personality disorder and their 2-month-old infants. *British Journal of Psychiatry, 183:* 239–247.

Epstein, R. A. (1990). Assessment and suitability for low-fee control psychoanalysis. *Journal of the American Psychoanalytic Association, 38:* 951–984.

Erie, J., & Goldberg, D. (1979). An approach to the study of analysability and analysis: The course of 40 consecutive cases selected for supervised analysis. *Psychoanalytic Quarterly, 47:* 198–228.

Fenichel, O. (1945). *The Psychoanalytic Theory of Neurosis*. New York: W. W. Norton.

Fonagy, P., Leigh, T., Steele, M., Steele, H., Kennedy, R., Mattoon, G., et al. (1996). The relation of attachment status, psychiatric classification, and response to psychotherapy. *Journal of Consulting and Clinical Psychology, 64:* 22–31.

Frank, J. (1956). Indications and contraindications for the standard technique. *Journal of the American Psychoanalytic Association, 4:* 266–284.

Freud, A. (1954). The widening scope of indications for psychoanalysis. *Journal of the American Psychoanalytic Association, 2:* 607–620. [Also in: *The Widening Scope of Indications for Analysis: Indications for Child Analysis*. London: Hogarth Press, 1969.]

Freud, S. (1904a). Freud's psycho-analytic procedure. *Standard Edition, 7:* 249–254.

Freud, S. (1905a). On psychotherapy. *Standard Edition, 7:* 257–268.

Freud, S. (1905e [1901]). Fragment of an analysis of a case of hysteria. *Standard Edition, 7:* 7–122.

Freud, S. (1912b). The dynamics of transference. *Standard Edition, 12:* 99–108.

Freud, S. (1912e). Recommendations to physicians practising psychoanalysis. *Standard Edition, 12:* 111–120.

Freud, S. (1915b). Thoughts for the times on war and death. *Standard Edition, 14:* 273–302.

Freud, S. (1917e [1915]). Mourning and melancholia. *Standard Edition, 14:* 243–258.

Freud, S. (1920g). *Beyond the Pleasure Principle. Standard Edition*, 18: 7–64.

Freud, S. (1921c). *Group Psychology and the Analysis of the Ego. Standard Edition*, 18: 69–143.

Freud, S. (1926d [1925]). *Inhibitions, Symptoms and Anxiety. Standard Edition*, 20: 77–175.

Freud, S. (1937c). Analysis terminable and interminable. *Standard Edition*, 23: 216–253.

Garelick, A. (1994). Psychotherapy assessment: Theory and practice. *Psychoanalytic Psychotherapy, 8* (2): 101–116.

Garland, C. (Ed.) (1998). *Understanding Trauma: A Psychoanalytic Approach.* Tavistock Clinic Series. London: Duckworth [revised edition, London: Karnac, 2002).

Garland, C. (2005). Trauma and the possibility of recovery. In: S. Budd & R. Rusbridger (Eds.), *Introducing Psychoanalysis: Essential Themes and Topics* (pp. 246–263). London: Routledge.

George, C., Kaplan, N., & Main, M. (1985). *The Adult Attachment Interview for Adults* (2nd edition). Unpublished manuscript, University of California, Berkeley, CA.

Glover, E. (1954). The indications for psychoanalysis. *Journal of Mental Science, 100:* 393–401.

Greenson, R. R. (1967). *The Technique and Practice of Psycho-Analysis, Vol. 1.* London: Hogarth Press.

Herman, J. (1992). *Trauma and Recovery: From Domestic Abuse to Political Terror.* New York: Basic Books.

Hesse, E., & Main, M. (2006). Frightened, threatening and dissociative parental behaviour in low-risk samples: Description, discussion, and interpretations. *Development and Psychopathology, 18*: 309–343.

Hinshelwood, R. D. (1995). Psychodynamic formulation in assessment for psychoanalytic psychotherapy. In: C. Mace (Ed.), *The Art and Science of Assessment in Psychotherapy* (pp. 155–166). London: Routledge.

Hobson, R. F. (1985). *Forms of Feeling: The Heart of Psychotherapy.* London: Routledge.

Hobson, R. P. (1985). Self-representing dreams. *Psychoanalytic Psychotherapy, 1* (3): 43–53 [reprinted 2008, *Psychoanalytic Psychotherapy, 22*: 20–30].

Hobson, R. P. (1993). The emotional origins of social understanding. *Philosophical Psychology, 6*: 227–249.

Hobson, R. P. (2002). *The Cradle of Thought.* London: Macmillan; New York: Oxford University Press, 2004.

Hobson, R. P., & Kapur, R. (2005). Working in the transference: Clinical and research perspectives. *Psychology & Psychotherapy: Theory, Research and Practice, 78*: 1–21.

Hobson, R. P., Patrick, M. P. H., Crandell, L., Garcia-Pérez, R., & Lee, A. (2005). Personal relatedness and attachment in infants of mothers with borderline personality disorder. *Development and Psychopathology, 17,* 329–347.

Hobson, R. P., Patrick, M., Hobson, J. A., Crandell, L., Bronfman, E., & Lyons-Ruth, K. (2009). How mothers with borderline personality disorder relate to their infants. *British Journal of Psychiatry, 195*: 325–330.

Hobson, R. P., Patrick, M. P. H., & Valentine, J. D. (1998). Objectivity in psychoanalytic judgements. *British Journal of Psychiatry, 173*: 172–177.

Hoglend, P., Amlo, S., Marble, A., Bogwald, K.-P., Sorbye, O., Sjaastad, M. C., et al. (2006). Analysis of the patient–therapist relationship in dynamic psychotherapy: An experimental study of transference interpretations. *American Journal of Psychiatry, 163*: 1739–1746.

Huxster, H., Lower, R., & Escott, P. (1975). Some pitfalls in assessment of analyzability in a psychoanalytic clinic. *Journal of the American Psychoanalytic Association, 23*: 90–106.

Jones, E. (1920). *Treatment of Neuroses.* London: Bailliere, Tindall & Cox.

Joseph, B. (1985). Transference: The total situation. In: *Psychic Equilibrium and Psychic Change* (pp. 157–168). London: Routledge, 1989.

Kantrowitz, J. (1987). Suitability for psychoanalysis. In: R. Langs (Ed.), *The Yearbook of Psychoanalysis and Psychotherapy* (pp. 403–416). New York: Gardner.

Kantrowitz, J., Katz, A. L., Greenhan, D., Morris, H., Paolitto, F., Sashin, O., et al. (1989). The patient–analyst match and the outcome of psychoanalysis: A pilot study. *Journal of the American Psychoanalytic Association, 37*: 893–920.

Kapur, R. (1998). *The Effects of Different Styles of Interpretation on the State of Mind of the Patient in Individual Psychotherapy.* Unpublished PhD thesis, Birkbeck College, University of London.

Kernberg, O., Burnstein, E., Coyne, L., Appelbaum, A., Horowitz, L., & Voth, H. (1972). Psychotherapy and psychoanalysis. Final part of the Menninger Foundation's psychotherapy research project. *Bulletin of the Menninger Clinic, 36*: 1–275.

Klauber, J. (1971). Personal attitudes to psychoanalytic consultation. In: *Difficulties in the Analytic Encounter* (pp. 141–159). New York: Jason Aronson, 1981.

Klein, M. (1935). A contribution to the psychogenesis of manic-depressive states. *International Journal of Psychoanalysis, 16*: 282–310.

Klein, M. (1946). Notes on some schizoid mechanisms. *International Journal of Psychoanalysis. 27*: 99–110.

Klein, M. (1952). The origins of transference. In: *The Writings of Melanie Klein, Vol. 3* (pp. 48–56). London: Hogarth Press, 1975.

Knapp, P. H., Levin, S., McCarter, R. H., Wetment, H., & Zetzel, E. (1960). Suitability for psychoanalysis: A review of one hundred supervised analytic cases. *Psychoanalytic Quarterly, 29*: 459–477.

Kohon, G. (1986). *The British School of Psychoanalysis: The Independent Tradition*. London: Free Association Books.

Liberman, D. (1968). Comment on Dr Waldhorn's paper. *International Journal of Psychoanalysis, 48:* 362–363.

Limentani, A. (1972). The assessment of analysability: A major hazard in selection for psychoanalysis. In: *Between Freud and Klein* (pp. 50–72). London: Free Association Books, 1989.

Lyons-Ruth, K., Melnick, S., Patrick, M. P. H., & Hobson, R. P. (2007). A controlled study of Hostile-Helpless states of mind among borderline and dysthymic women. *Attachment and Human Development, 9:* 1–16.

Lyons-Ruth, K., Yellin, C., Melnick, S., & Atwood, G. (2005). Expanding the concept of unresolved mental states: Hostile/Helpless states of mind on the Adult Attachment Interview are associated with atypical behaviour and infant disorganization. *Development and Psychopathology, 17:* 1–23.

Mace, C. (Ed.) (1995). *The Art and Science of Assessment in Psychotherapy*. London: Routledge.

Maslow, A. (1954). *Motivation and Personality*. New York: Harper & Row.

Namnum, R. (1968). The problem of analysability and the autonomous ego. *International Journal of Psychoanalysis, 49:* 271–275.

Ogden, T. H. (1989). *The Primitive Edge of Experience*. London: Karnac.

Ogden, T. H. (2002). A new reading of the origins of object-relations theory. *International Journal of Psychoanalysis, 83:* 767–782.

Patrick, M. P. H., Hobson, R. P., Castle, D., Howard, R., & Maughan, B. (1994). Personality disorder and the mental representation of early social experience. *Development and Psychopathology, 6:* 375–388.

Piper, W. E., Azim, H. F. A., Joyce, A. S., & McCallum, M. (1991). Transference interpretations, therapeutic alliance, and outcome in short-term individual psychotherapy. *Archives of General Psychiatry, 48:* 946–953.

Pollock, G. H. (1960). The role and responsibilities of the psychoanalytic consultant. *International Journal of Psychoanalysis, 41:* 633–636.

Racker, H. (1968). *Transference and Countertransference*. London: Hogarth Press [reprinted London: Karnac, 1982].

Reich, W. (1933). *Character Analysis*. London: Vision, 1950.

Riesenberg-Malcolm, R. (1995). The three "W"s: What, where and when: The rationale of interpretation. *International Journal of Psychoanalysis, 76:* 447–456.

Roth, P. (2001). Mapping the landscape: Levels of transference interpretation. *International Journal of Psychoanalysis, 82:* 533–543.

Sandler, J. I., Holder, A., Kawenoka, M., Kennedy, H. E., & Neurath, L. (1969). Notes on some theoretical and clinical aspects of transference. *International Journal of Psychoanalysis, 50:* 633–645.

Sashin, J. I., Eldred, S. H., & Van Amerongen, S. T. (1975). A search for predictive factors in institute supervised cases: A retrospective study of 183 cases from 1959–1966 at the Boston Psychoanalytic Society & Institute. *International Journal of Psychoanalysis, 56:* 343–359.

Schubart, W. (1989). The patient in the psychoanalyst's consulting room: The first consultation as a psychoanalytic encounter. *International Journal of Psychoanalysis, 70:* 423–432.

Sebold, A. (1999). *Lucky.* London: Picador.

Sebold, A. (2003). *The Lovely Bones.* London: Picador.

Segal, H. (1957). Notes on symbol formation. *International Journal of Psychoanalysis, 38:* 391–397.

Shapiro, S. (1984). The initial assessment of the patient: A psychoanalytic approach. *International Review of Psychoanalysis, 11:* 11–25.

Stone, L. (1954). The widening scope of indications for psychoanalysis. *Journal of the American Psychoanalytic Association, 2:* 567–594.

Strachey, J. B. (1934). The nature of the therapeutic action of psycho-analysis. *International Journal of Psychoanalysis, 15:* 127–159.

Thompson, C. (1938). Notes on the psychoanalytic significance of the choice of analyst. *Psychoanalytic Quarterly, 29:* 205–216.

Tyson, R. L., & Sandler, J. (1971). Problems in the selection of patients for psychoanalysis: Comments on the application of the concepts of "indications", "suitability" and "analysability". *British Journal of Medical Psychology, 44:* 211–228.

van der Kolk, B. A. (2005). Developmental trauma disorder. *Psychiatric Annals, 35:* 401–408.

Vygotsky, L. S. (1978). Internalization of higher psychological functions. In: M. Cole, V. John-Steiner, S. Scribner, & E. Souberman (Eds.), *Mind in Society: The Development of Higher Psychological Processes* (pp. 52–57). Cambridge, MA: Harvard University Press.

Waldhorn, H. F. (1960). Assessment of analysability: Technical and theoretical observations. *Psychoanalytic Quarterly, 29:* 478–506.

Waldhorn, H. F. (1968). Indications and contraindications: Lessons from the second analysis. *International Journal of Psychoanalysis, 49:* 358–362.

Weissman, M. M., Markowitz, J. C., & Klerman, G. L. (2007). *Clinician's Quick Guide to Interpersonal Psychotherapy.* Oxford: Oxford University Press.

Winnicott, D. W. (1964). *The Child, the Family, and the Outside World.* Harmondsworth: Penguin.

Zetzel, E. (1965). The theory of therapy in relation to a developmental model of the psychic apparatus. *International Journal of Psychoanalysis, 46:* 39–52.

Zetzel, E. (1968). The so-called good hysteric. In: *The Capacity for Emotional Growth* (pp. 229–245). New York: International Universities Press, 1970 [reprinted London: Karnac, 1987].

INDEX

For Product Safety Concerns and Information please contact our EU
representative GPSR@taylorandfrancis.com
Taylor & Francis Verlag GmbH, Kaufingerstraße 24, 80331 München, Germany

www.ingramcontent.com/pod-product-compliance
Lightning Source LLC
Chambersburg PA
CBHW070404270326
41926CB00014B/2699